Tales From The Curio Cabinet

MARJIE ZACKS

Tales from the Curio Cabinet
Copyright 2023 Marjie Zacks

No part of this publication may be reproduced or transmitted in any form or by any means, electronic or mechanical, including photocopying, recording or for any information storage and retrieval system, now known or to be invented, without permission in writing from the publisher.

Published by Marjie Zacks
Contact: mszacks53@gmail.com
ISBN 978-1-7782553-2-8 (softcover)
ISBN 978-1-7782553-3-5 (eBook)

Edited by: Marial Shea
Cover and text design by: Tania Craan
eBook produced by: Jan Westendorp

CONTENTS

Introduction 7

The Bottom Shelf — *The Growing-Up Years* 9

Valentine's Day 11

Sweet and sorrow 14

My father's tallit 18

Miss Strickland 22

Stewed prunes 26

Horowitz is a good name 29

The Middle Shelf — *Trials and Tribulations* 33

The continuing saga of the parfait glasses 35

When you're miserable, throw a party 38

The curio cabinet approves again 41

Aging, a stealthy adversary 44

Masking our senses ... if we have any to begin with 46

There's a reason we have more than one friend 48

Why must we live up to others' expectations? 50

A true sense of accomplishment 52

Two nights before Passover 55

Rules and laws are for honest people 58

I'll do it my own self! Three-year-olds have the right idea 61

Communication is a wonderful thing 65

Communications age, indeed! 68

Collateral benefits of renovation 71

Rising to the occasion 75

Undercover spies 80

The Top Shelf — *Aging Is Not for Sissies* 83

Lasting impressions 85

The mystery of the QR code 87

Aging, the funny side 90

Either too young or too old 93

Buried treasure 96

Goodbye Red River, gone but not forgotten 99

Passing the torch *or* when will kids take on the holidays? 101

The perfect birthday present 105

Oh goodie, a brand-new fire-engine-red ... Rollator! 108

We can't take ourselves too seriously *or* get out the scissors 111

It's about those shoes 114

Aging gracefully 117

The graying of Canada 120

The doctor's appointment 123

The leopard never changes its spots, unless you ask nicely 127

Bikini beach 129

"I don't buy green bananas" 133

Speaking of legacies 136

Not yet 139

Is it pajama time yet? 142

The value of an experiential learner 145

A final thought on aging, a curiosity all its own 148

Acknowledgements 151

About the Author 153

Introduction

In my first book, *It All Ends Up in a Parfait Glass*, I wrote about the lessons I learned from the funny expressions and sayings my mom used when I was growing up. Now that I am older, I realize just how much her wisdom contributed to who I am today. I also realize that, as a "very young senior" (as I call myself) with considerable life experience, I no longer need to borrow the opinions of others. I know myself pretty well. After all, I have been hanging out with me my whole life.

I believe that, like cheese and wine, we get better with age. At least, let's hope so. Any lessons our parents left out, life teaches us along the way. With any luck, twenty-twenty hindsight will save us from repeating the follies of our younger days.

Of course, follies are not limited to our youth. I don't know about you, but I certainly have many funny stories to tell about aging. Seniors, both young and old, view the world from a new vantage point. Although I started this book by writing about the mystery of my mother's curio cabinet, I moved on to capturing my world in what turned out to be three main areas. I like to think of them as shelves in the curio cabinet. On the bottom shelf, I acknowledge The Growing-Up Years and the influence they had on me. The middle shelf is about coping with the adversities life has thrown my way — my Trials and Tribulations. And, on the top shelf I offer my observations of life from a new vantage point, my perch at the other end of the age spectrum. As I have been warned many times by those who have gone before me, Aging Is Not for Sissies

Who knew that a curio(sity) cabinet is called this because it is a place to show off one's curiosities or miniatures, special mementos, gifts, keepsakes and treasures that have significant meaning? I am hoping you share in some of these curiosities I've gathered over a lifetime, and that you enjoy reading about them as much as I enjoyed the writing.

How curious life is. What's in your curio cabinet?

Here's what's in mine.

The Bottom Shelf

The Growing-Up Years

Valentine's Day

When we were children, Valentine's Day, although not something we were supposed to celebrate in the Jewish community, was a time we were reminded just how much we were loved. Our parents brought us little treats, always a card and sometimes a little gift, such as a handkerchief. As time went on, and because we had been taught that it was not just about receiving but giving, we would reciprocate. A special card. A small token of our love for our parents.

As we got older, we became aware that Valentine's Day was a big deal for boyfriends and girlfriends, and even husbands and wives. My dad always had a beautiful card for my mom and she always had one for him. I know. I found them all when I was going through my mom's many boxes after she passed away. Oh, the guilt of throwing all those cards away! But who else were they for? In fact, looking at them felt a bit like spying.

Valentine's Day at home was a great chance to express our love for family, while at school we had the competition to see who got the most Valentines from classmates. Not being terribly popular, I was delighted to get one or two and then always one from a secret admirer. My close friend who lived across the road always brought me a Valentine and I had one for him too.

Naturally, over the years I would give and receive Valentines, always getting a card from my parents, and when my dad passed away, from my mom. She would buy me a red sweater or scarf or mitts, just a token to mark the day, and I always bought her a little something. I passed on the tradition with my own daughter and then my acquired sons. Always a card and perhaps a gift for my daughter. Boys aren't too keen on Valentines from a step-mom once they get to a certain age, but they were always happy to receive a bag of Valentine's candy. To this day my husband and I go out for dinner to celebrate our love for each other.

We soon had another reason to celebrate on Valentine's Day. Our dog, Smurf, a gift from my mom, was born on February 13th. We always made a Valentine-themed party for him on his birthday. White cupcakes for all, as doggies can't eat chocolate. I always included my mom and one of her friends in our doggie party. We all put on party hats, dog included, and sang and had a great time. Of course, when my husband first came on the scene, he thought we were lunatics. Though the years confirmed it, guess who took to wearing a party hat along with us?

For many years after my mom passed away, and for as long as Smurf lived, we continued to hold a birthday party for him inviting my mom's friends, who were now in their hundred-plus years and had partaken of earlier celebrations. Sadly, Smurf only made it to fifteen years of age. Of course, that is a hundred and five in human years, so he had as much stamina as that generation of my mom's friends.

At a certain age, my daughter pointed out to me that a Valentine from a mom to a daughter was no longer the thing to do. If it didn't come from that special guy, it wasn't valid. Okay, then. I guess I would stick with the bag of candy. And then that tradition just went by the wayside. Fortunately, there are now three grandchildren, whom I love to spoil with candy hearts and cards. What's so wrong with having a tradition where you express love for the ones who matter to you? Does it have to be a dating relationship to count?

What do I know, I am old school. I like the tradition and I'm sticking to it. You don't like it? Don't eat the candy. Your dentist will probably prefer that, anyway. I'm not bringing him anything sweet when I see him to replace my latest nightguard, which I have ground through completely.

Happy Valentine's Day.

Sweet and sorrow

There my mother sat at the kitchen table, eating a piece of blueberry cake and sobbing her eyes out. At the age of twelve, I had not developed the insight and empathy to understand how the taste of something wonderful could bring back memories and trigger so much sorrow.

When I was growing up I had only two grandparents, my mother's parents, who lived in Boston. My father's parents were gone by the time I was born. In fact, I was named for my paternal grandfather, Moishe Shmuel. How strange that name sounds in English: Moses Samuel. I never referred to him by his English name, although I did try to convince our rabbi who taught Hebrew School that my name was not really Musha Sima, the female derivative of his name in Hebrew, but rather the much more attractive sounding Miriam. He just smiled patiently and said, "Okay. Miriam it is." Little did I know that my grandfather was probably on the hiring committee when our rabbi was brought to our small community to lead our congregation. Also, the rabbi was a patient of my father's and would do anything to keep his family physician's daughter happy.

By the time I came along, I only had one set of grandparents. What were they doing in the United States? Oh, pretty much what they did every day in their home in the Boston area. My mom was born there and was American. My dad was Canadian. Every summer and most holidays, we would get on an airplane and fly to New York, then switch planes to fly to Boston to visit our Bobi and Zadie, as we called them. They were these older people who seemed to love us a lot and were very important to our mother, so we went along with it. One story was told about my Bobi having run out of something and dashing out to the store while my sister was eating breakfast. When she came back, Bobi found my sister eating the white butter as if it were cheese. In Canada our butter was yellow, but it was white in the U.S., so my sister thought she was eating cream cheese. How was she to know?

We didn't know our grandparents very well. I have few memories of them except for riding the subway with my grandmother when I was maybe ten years old. She was talking very loudly, as she was hard of hearing. I was embarrassed. Little did I know how I would regret my embarrassment a short time later.

The phone rang. It was a Saturday morning in late August, that glorious time when camp was over and school had yet to start. Maybe five or six whole days to just be. My Uncle Sam, my mother's brother from Boston, was on the other end of the line. Did we know where "mother" was?

How could we know where Bobi was when we were hundreds of miles north, in Canada?

The milk bottles were still on her doorstep when Uncle Sam went to check on her. No one seemed to know where she was, and by late afternoon my mother was as frantic as my uncle.

Finally, late that evening, my uncle went to the morgue. There he found my grandmother.

Her body had been brought in following an accident. Saturday was the one day our Bobi went to *shul* (synagogue). On this Saturday, she walked to shul as always with no purse. What would she need it for, she was going to pray. Apparently she stepped out into the street to avoid a fallen tree and was hit by a speeding car. No one knew who she was because she carried no identification. Further, she had been struck so hard that when my mother arrived on the scene the next day, she discovered her mother's shoe still caught up in a branch of the tree.

I remember this as a very sad time. My mother was devastated. Her mother was not much older than I am now. I guess they took care of everything and arranged a funeral. I was at home with some kind of very bad cold. Without my mom there to comfort me, I was miserable. Nor was I there to comfort her.

My mom brought back many things of her mother's. Most important of all was her famed recipe book. As a caterer, she had many wonderful recipes. I know, I have them today. And my mother, like my grandmother, was an incredible cook and baker. I remember my mother sitting at the kitchen table sobbing as she nibbled on blueberry cake, which she noted was the last such cake my grandmother would ever make. I can only imagine how that must have felt.

Today, as a grown up (so they say), I have a pretty good idea how she felt eating the last of the blueberry cake. Every time I make my mother's special Bundt cake it brings back all kinds of good memories of my mom. I am especially pleased when it turns out just like she made it — not an easy feat and one that I accomplish only occasionally. Who would think that tasting something sweet could trigger so much sadness along with wonderful memories? I think of my mom, just as she thought of hers as she ate the last of her mother's blueberry cake.

My father's tallit

Many Jewish kids grow up like I did, going to synagogue, where we stand next to our fathers, who are wearing a prayer shawl or *tallit* and a *kippah* (yarmulke) on their heads. When the service gets long and boring and the rabbi drones on and on in what seems like a never-ending sermon, we might take to twirling the *tzitzit* (tassels) on our father's tallit just to pass the time. It's a comforting silky feel, and since it was rare for women to wear a tallit, this was a father-child thing.

Long after my father passed away, I came across his tallit bag and tallit. The velvet was old and worn and had clearly sat in the window where the blue had faded to almost green. The tallit was wrinkled but still clean — white and blue. Back in the day, the prayer shawl was about a foot wide, not huge and all-encompassing as many men and some women wear today. Perhaps they think the bigger the tallit, the more religious they appear. Some of these tallits are so big they can often double as the canopy or *chupa* at the wedding of son or daughter. At a diminutive five foot four, my dad would be swallowed whole in such a tallit if he were alive today.

So often over the years, moving from one house to another, digging through cupboards while I hunted for this or that, my dad's tallit would appear. He had no boys to pass it on to, so I guess it was left to me. I never knew what to do with it, so I would put it back in the bag, along with his Passover *Haggadah* (prayer book), and promptly forget where I put it.

Not long ago, a dear friend and I were out for dinner with our significant others. Hers mentioned a young Jewish doctor who had come from a part of the world where being Jewish was not looked upon with favour. Only here in Canada could he now discover his roots and learn how to pray. As he didn't have a tallit, he was looking for one. I said I would be happy to give him my father's.

Then I thought, what if someday my daughter has a son? Maybe this wasn't such a good offer. And, of course, when I went to find the tallit it was nowhere to be seen. What on earth did I do with it? They always say that you find things when you are looking for something else. Sure enough, I was looking for Chanukah decorations from last year when, down in the basement on a bookshelf, what should I discover but my father's tallit? In fact, as I opened the bag I discovered two tallits. Had it been my bag all along, I would say there were two tallits because I am a Gemini, but my dad was a Scorpio so why would he have two? That is a mystery all its own, but it meant I could be a good citizen and offer one to the Jewish doctor (if all these weeks later he still needed one) and one to keep in case my daughter ever has a son.

I told my sister about the tallits and she also had no clue why there were two. However, she did say she would wear the tallit if there was no male heir in the family. Times have changed and now that's perfectly acceptable. In fact, I think our dad would be touched and honoured.

It was still a mystery why there were two tallits in the bag. My uncle had had sons and grandsons so it did not make sense that the second one would be his. Maybe these prayer shawls multiply if left alone long enough? No, that couldn't be it. Well, at least I know where the tallits are now. It's a sentimental attachment, for sure, but they and my dad's binoculars are pretty much all I have of him now. I will treasure them.

The story does not end here, however. I took my father's tallit to a dry cleaner, a special one located in a plaza in a Jewish neighbourhood. I was told they would know how to clean it properly, carefully, delicately and, most importantly, without untying the knots, which have religious significance. When I said to the woman behind the counter, "You do know how to clean this, right? You won't untie the knots?" she laughed and told me that is an old Italian joke. Not really. It is an old Jewish joke, but maybe she was Italian and wanted pride of ownership. Either way, it's a good joke. I gave her my first and last names and left.

Seems the last laugh was on me. When I came back for the clean tallit, she asked my name again. There, on the sales slip attached to the plastic, was my last name, but with my father's first initial. Who says there are no coincidences in life? My father must have had his tallit cleaned here before, or at least had something cleaned at this very dry cleaner, because there was his initial "L" instead of my "M." Was this a message from above, telling me I had made a good decision in passing my father's tallit on to someone who was finally able to re-establish his Jewish roots? Or was this just a quirky kind of happenstance? I checked my keyboard and the L and the M are near each other. Is it simply a mistake or do I take it as a message from beyond? I choose the latter. Who says our parents aren't with us for the rest of our lives?

P.S. When I finally offered this clean, well-used and much-loved tallit through my friend's partner to his colleague, I was told there was no way this one would do. Turned out the new Canadian was broad shouldered and about six foot five inches. Oh well. My sister was thrilled to have that tallit. I still have the other — somewhere. Now, where did I put it?

Miss Strickland

As life's rites of passage go, this was a strange one. She was the guardian at the gate through which you must pass if you were ever going to have a life beyond Grade 5. Looking back at the fear with which she ruled her fiefdom, it was a wonder any of us ended up unscathed. First there was the door that had to be closed quietly, never slammed. Quirkily, it would not remain closed unless you rotated the handle a half turn to the left and then another quarter turn to the right and pulled it closed just so. She seated us in rows based on our marks, so the brightest child was next to the door (a place I would never inhabit). It was a year to be survived.

Miss Strickland wasn't any ordinary elementary school teacher. She was old. She was so old she was ancient. She had been at Queen Elizabeth Public School from the Dark Ages. And she was stricter than anyone we had ever met. Our siblings, upon hearing who our teacher for that year would be, trembled, "Uh-oh. Good luck."

The old battle axe, as she was labelled by some, was known for having two desks, one at the front of the class and one at the back. She had eyes in the back of her head, and before she pounced, she would draw on her innate sense of who wanted to be picked on least.

We were allotted a new pencil every month. The colours matched the seasons — yellow for September, orange for October, green for November and red for December. It was a very traumatic year for me. It was the first time we were allowed to write in ink, and we had these weird pens with two bumps where our fingers should be positioned, and darned if old Ma Strickland couldn't tell when you were holding your pen wrong from clear across the room.

I have a distinct memory of her using her middle finger torpedoing straight down onto my head to make a point. "I saw you holding your pen improperly at 10:15." Who, me? It's almost lunchtime! The girls all started to wear headbands for protection. Not the plastic ones to keep hair out of your face because such was the force of her finger that those headbands broke; no, we chose the soft ones to add protective padding, just in case.

She was quite a task master, assigning homework and never letting you forget that you had not finished your math questions left over from two weeks ago Thursday. She had everyone's name written in a long list of unfinished business (in those days in long hand) so that as soon as you finally finished one piece of work, she was harping on what still had to be done. When you finally finished, you could go pick a book from her little library, but of course the back of the book had questions to be answered to determine just how much you had comprehended. Not once did I get past the first question, let alone the first book, from September to year's end.

I will never forget how stuck I was on a math question. You weren't allowed to move on from that homework until it was done to perfection. No matter what I did, I could not figure it out. Even the paperboy, who happened to be in my class, couldn't help me. There was nothing for it. I pretended to be sick to stay in at recess so I could copy someone else's work (from the row to the right where the smarter kids sat, never to the left), but Miss Strickland marched in just as I was finally getting the answer down. That cost me ten more questions. When she called us row by row to report to the back desk, I was quaking in my shoes. From her perch, she announced to the class, "You cheated and you still couldn't get it right." It was not a good year. The best part of the year for me was catching pneumonia when trick or treating on Hallowe'en and having to stay in bed for four weeks. Four whole weeks away from that teacher.

Of course, that was the year we started public speaking with impromptu one-minute speeches. Pure terror. Getting up in front of the class and supposedly talking about your pet peeve — was that a bird? I hadn't a clue. I was only ten and had skipped a year, so what did I know?

Every morning began with "God Save the Queen" — imagine — followed by getting out our health notebooks where we had a checklist of all the habits we were to be learning, including being in bed by 8 p.m., brushing our hair and teeth and showering every day. (That was never going to happen.) We had to have a clean hanky at all times. I just kept mine in the health book in my desk and it was always neatly pressed. Of course, it was never used. Woe betide anyone with dirty fingernails. They were sent to the janitor's closet with a bar of soap and a brush. Who keeps that in their desk?

Then came Bible reading. Always from the Old Testament. A bizarre concept of education indeed. And yet everyone at

Queen Elizabeth School had to go through Miss Strickland's class. I'm sure there were the lucky ones who didn't, but I didn't know any of them.

At Christmas, it was rumoured that Miss Strickland gave out a bag of candy to each class member and actually wished us all a good holiday. That part turned out to be true.

Looking back on that year I can still feel the fear of putting up my hand to answer a question and praying she would choose someone else. What we didn't know until close to the end of the school year was that this was her retirement year. At age sixty-five, retirement in those days was mandatory. Her reign of terror was coming to an end. No future generations would suffer. I could also see why it would be a hard year for her knowing it would be her last one in the classroom. She must have wanted to get the most out of it. So many students in what was at least a forty-five-year career. They said she was a good teacher and if you made it through you were good to go, but I don't remember learning much of anything that year. Wait, that's not completely true. I learned that the word execution meant having your head cut off. The only time Miss Strickland was impressed was when during a history lesson she asked who knew another word for beheading. Funny that execution was the word I knew. Freud would have a field day.

Stewed prunes

Why do some impressions last a lifetime and others do not? Fifty-seven years after I was in Grade 7 and 8, I can still tell you all about how I spent my time failing home economics. Yes, in those days Grade 7 and 8 students went from our elementary school, which had no kitchens, and no woodworking or metal shop, to a school even further away than the high school we would be attending in short order. This school was in what was known as East City and we lived in the west part of town. Every Tuesday we would go first to our school for attendance, reciting the Lord's Prayer and singing "God Save the Queen." Then we would all troop across town, past the downtown core and the high school, up a huge hill, to this other school for the girls to learn how to sew and cook and the boys to do woodworking and metal work.

Now, if I could have taken manual training, as it was called then, instead of home economics, I would have done fine. I had no interest in, and even less talent for, sewing and I was not much better at cooking. Many students' moms had sewing machines. My mom did not. So, when an assignment was given in Grade 7 to make an apron, all my classmates could go home and have their moms show them how to use the sewing machine and finish off the apron. But for me, there was no point in discussing this challenge with my mom. My sister spoke up and was taken to the dressmaker to help her through home economics, but I kept my mouth shut. I just dreaded Tuesday mornings until high school began.

On the first day of class, we began working on a bag. Mine was red. What was to go in this burlap bag I have no idea, but it had to have our initials on the outside and a lining on the inside. The bag was very complex to me; by the time everyone else was finished their very professional looking bags, I was still trying to sort out the lining for mine. They all went on to make blouses.

For some reason the teacher picked me as the model for how to make a blouse. When it got to measuring the darts, I was so mortified I turned the same shade as my red bag. There was no removing of clothes, thankfully, but having a teacher that close to me, encircling my ever-so-unimpressive body with her measuring tape, was humiliating. To make matters worse, after sacrificing my body, literally, I had to return to finishing the red bag of disaster. By the time I finished, the semester was almost over.

There was no time left for me to start on a blouse. Fine. My next assignment would be another bag in a different fabric, this time pink and see through. When I finally managed to assemble the thing, I had to iron it. Apparently the iron was far too hot and I scorched the bag beyond redemption, leaving most of it on the iron's surface. I was now definitely on the teacher's hit list. Fine with me. Bags had been my nemesis all year, and this one was now so diminished that only one shoe would fit in it.

The cooking part of home economics was even more of a puzzle. We learned to make stewed prunes, just what every twelve and thirteen-year-old was craving that year for sure. I guess they thought that someday, when we got to be the age of the teacher, we would be grateful. Never have I ever made stewed prunes, to this day. But should anyone need any tutelage in this endeavour, do get in touch with me. Though I left Grade 8 without a clue how to sew or cook by the teacher's standards, I have never forgotten this particular dish.

Thankfully, I had access to dressmakers and marvelous cookbooks and a mom who was an ace in the kitchen. She left me in good shape with her cooking legacy. And someday I just may appreciate those stewed prunes.

Horowitz is a good name

There's an old story about a Jewish immigrant coming to North America and trying to blend in at a time when antisemitism was common. Many Jews arrived at Ellis Island with names that were not only long, but derived from the Yiddish word for what their family did for a living or where they lived. Rosenberg is a rose on a hill. Shvartz or Shwartz meant the family worked as Blacksmiths. Some names weren't so easy to pronounce unless you were fluent in Yiddish, Polish or German.

Part of our family ended up in Israel. One summer they came to Canada for an extended visit to see our grandparents. When the summer ended and it came time for kids to return to school, my grandparents decided to enroll my eleven-year-old Israeli cousin in Grade 5. My cousin's name was Tzipora (Tzippy for short), which in Hebrew means bird. However, my grandparents thought her classmates and teacher would have a hard time pronouncing her name, so they enrolled her as Frances. Why Frances? It sounded so not Jewish. It sounded Canadian. How bizarre is that?

What's in a name? A lot. When immigrants with long, unpronounceable last names arrived in Saint John, New Brunswick, or Montreal, Quebec, and especially in New York or New Jersey, names were often shortened for ease of pronunciation and to save the time it would take to record all those convoluted syllables. Rosenberg became Rosen, Schwartzenheimer became Swartz, and so on.

But there was another reason so many Jewish folk chose to Anglicize their names. That was to blend in.

As my "Aunt Louise" told this story, one such Jewish fellow wanted to change his name so badly that he got himself before a judge and pleaded. "Mr. Shonenburg, what did you have in mind for your new name?" inquired the judge. To which Mr. Shonenburg replied in his heavily accented English, "I'm tanking [thinking] and tanking. I'm tanking Horowitz is a good name."

How does that expression go? The more things change, the more they stay the same? I loved that story. I chuckled every time I thought of the new Mr. Horowitz. He chose a name just as Jewish as his own, but somehow it made him feel more American. Fitting in was always what we wanted most, a sense of belonging with everyone else. That's called assimilation. Back then everyone wanted to fit in and belong — to become Canadian. Now it seems we are busy focusing on everyone's differences instead of what we all have in common. But I digress.

Aunt Louise was not really my aunt. She was a longtime friend and law school colleague of my mom's. We called her Aunt Louise as a sign of respect for elders who were almost family. Today we are lucky if we get called by our first names, never mind Mr., Ms., Miss or Mrs. A friend's young grandson has been taught by his nanny that all people are to be addressed as Miss or Mr. and then their first name. The first time this five-year-old addressed me as Miss Marjie I nearly fell over. I thought, now there is a polite young man.

What's in a name? A lot. Especially when it is your own.

The Middle Shelf

Trials and Tribulations

The continuing saga of the parfait glasses

I believe my mother is always watching over me, in a benevolent, good-spirit way. What more proof do I need than her curio cabinet, which she passed down to me. Some of her precious pieces of china live there, along with her cherished Lalique Birds and the special camels from my own extensive collection. But the wondrous thing about the curio cabinet is how it seems to open at the most appropriate times.

On the day I hosted a high tea for my friends, I decided to use my mother's beautiful strawberry dish, complete with sugar bowl and creamer. It seemed like the perfect container for the blueberry scones and clotted cream and jam I planned to serve along with party sandwiches and iced tea. There I was in my dining room, looking in the wall unit for this lovely Wedgewood piece. As soon as my hand reached for it, the curio cabinet door opened as if my mother was saying, "Good choice. Glad to see you are finally using my china." It opened again as I reached for the Wedgewood knives.

I have become so used to this spontaneous opening of the curio cabinet door that I just say, "Hi Mom," and go over to close it with the key. To this day, the door swings open on all the special occasions when there are guests at our table. Is this a coincidence? Who knows! My mother-in-law, still a going concern at age ninety-three, was totally spooked by this notion, even though she used to caution us to step right foot first when getting on a plane and would never walk between two people, as it was bad luck. The look on her face when I told her this story was priceless.

Back to the mysterious openings of the curio cabinet door. I was preparing a traditional apple cake for the Jewish High Holidays. Wanting to try a healthier version of the recipe, I substituted oat flour for two of the three cups of white flour. I had not realized that oat flour is quite a bit heavier than regular flour, requiring adjusting the oil and eggs to match. When I turned the tube pan over to cool the cake, it fell out in huge chunks. My mother, who was a fabulous cook and baker, would have thrown the mess out and started over.

Or maybe not. She might well have said, "Go get the parfait glasses," the solution to all problems in the kitchen (related in my previous book). A little whipped cream, a few berries and my mom would resurrect a disaster, turning it into a masterpiece. I looked at the mess on my kitchen counter and decided I, too, would get the parfait glasses. If only I had kept my mom's.

I went to my wall unit to see what I might use as a substitute. Lo and behold, there was the reason I hadn't taken my mom's parfait glasses: She had given me six of my own and I inherited another half dozen so long ago I had forgotten all about them. I was so thrilled that I immediately reached in and pulled them all out. At that moment, the curio cabinet door opened very quietly. I blessed my mom and her foresight. She knew I would need them someday.

The parfait dessert got rave reviews. My company was eating the disastrous apple cake, reincarnated! And wasn't that the best lesson my mom ever taught us? No matter what, make the best of it.

When you're miserable, throw a party

Covid had been going on for almost a year and a half when I finally climbed out of the doldrums. Then Delta showed up and threatened to wipe out the fall, including our youngest son's wedding. By that second Covid summer, we were able to enjoy distanced outdoor visits and a very occasional patio dinner, but it didn't feel normal. Just more Covid, only in warmer months. While it felt wonderful to step outside in t-shirt and shorts and to go swimming again, nothing was the way it used to be.

I was getting *very* tired of it.

So, I decided, what better way to cheer myself up than to throw a mini party. I invited two of my close friends and their husbands to join us for high tea. Was I doing the right thing in risking a pandemic party? Reassurance came when I pulled out my mother's strawberries-and-cream patterned dish, with its place for cream and sugar on either side. My friends commented on this treasured heirloom the minute they saw it, along with the Royal Crown Derby blue-and-white china-handled knives. As I was placing my homemade blueberry scones in the strawberry dish, I noticed that my mom's curio cabinet door had swung open by itself. That made twice this week, I thought, once when

I got out the strawberry dish and a second time when I got out the knives, both inherited from her. I felt so thrilled to know she approved.

I wanted some high-class touches for my high tea, in spite of the paper plates we had to use because of Covid. In advance, I had put the Devon cream in my mother's creamer and the raspberry jam in its sugar bowl. But when I asked my husband to bring out the cream from the fridge (the heat that day was scorching), what did he bring? The empty bottle I was keeping in case I had cream left over.

Heavy sigh. The kitchen is not a foreign country, yet my husband needs a road map to find anything there. He empties the dishwasher, a task he considers his, on a nightly basis, and mostly knows where things go, but send him into the fridge and he is hopelessly lost. "Never mind," my mother would say, "he has other great qualities," which is true.

When my mother first met my husband, she said, "He's wonderful. Such a nice man. Now I can die in peace."

"Oh, no, you can't. You're not going anywhere. I need you."

Thankfully, mindful of my protestations, she stuck around for four years pre-wedding and six years post. And on the day of my party, she was clearly looking down on me from somewhere she, too, could indulge in high tea. A very high tea. Did I mention that I am a wee bit addicted to high tea? And that it was my mom who introduced me to it?

My friends thanked us profusely for risking a backyard mini tea party. They loved the touches from my mother, and told me so. Coincidentally, one of my two invited friends (the one who had introduced me to my husband some twenty-two years before) was, that same night, observing *yahrzeit*, the anniversary of her mother's death. When she later called to say thanks, all of this brought emotion to her voice and tears to my eyes.

I have very little family, apart from a sister in California and cousins scattered across the U.S. and Israel. "Thanks for being my family," I said.

"Thanks for being mine," she replied.

This understanding that we can make anyone our "family" and support group has helped me during difficult times. They are there for me during celebrations too.

I'm so glad I found the courage that summer to say, "Enough is enough, I'm miserable. What I need is a party," and to set about putting one together on short notice.

The curio cabinet approves again

When my husband turned seventy, the birthday celebration seemed to have been going on all summer long. He called it the Birthday Era because there were about three weeks between his Hebrew birthday, or the birthday on the Hebraic calendar (that year was 5782) and his actual birthday on the English or Gregorian calendar.

First, there was a surprise weekend getaway where we golfed and relaxed at a resort up north. I managed to keep that a secret. Then there was dinner with his folks at our place for the Hebrew birthday. Then came the actual birthday, which fell on the first day of Rosh Hashanah, so, of course, we and the immediate family celebrated the night before at dinner. Finally, in the middle of the Jewish High Holidays, which come in rapid succession for what seems like a never-ending month or so, we held an expanded, extended family party. No friends, just family and more family — about thirty in all — in the backyard.

Would it rain? Should we rent a tent? What about a tarpaulin on top of the pergola that until now had seemed totally useless, except for hanging potted plants all summer and on which we and guests regularly bumped our heads? We had an awning over the back deck that would definitely help, but exactly how many people could we cram into that space and still maintain social distancing?

Thus, the night before the party, in a wind storm that had its own ideas, my husband and I were up on top of the pergola having a heated discussion about how to tie down the tarp. I said to him, "It's a darn good thing you work in solo practice. Your report card would definitely say 'Does not play well with others!'" In most circumstances, my husband is the exact opposite: he is charming, soft spoken, highly intelligent and socially astute to the point where he never puts a foot wrong and, unlike me, never puts it in his mouth. He has no enemies and never has a bad word to say about anyone except drivers who cut him off and cyclists who creep up behind us without using a bell. He is mostly laid back. Nevertheless, we had very different ideas of how to capture that tarp and get the hatches battened down. It made for an interesting time.

The morning of the party, skies were gloomy. It rained at 10. It rained at 11. It rained at 1. However, by the time the guests arrived at 2 p.m. the sun was shining and all was well. Had we not gone to all the trouble of putting up the tent, the awning and the tarp you can bet it would have poured. Oh well. These were our insurance policy. The event went off beautifully and I was grateful for good weather. My husband was so happy to celebrate with most of those he holds dear.

We had hired someone to staff the food table. His name was Charlie Brown. Really. He was lovely and very efficient. He even chatted up the guests, who were delighted by him. As we were tidying up, we came into the dining room and, sure enough, the curio cabinet was open. I guess this was my mom's way of telling me I had done a good job and a *mitzvah* (good deed) and that she approved. Poor Charlie. I told him the story of how the curio cabinet door never failed to open when I did the right thing. It was like moral reassurance from beyond — my mom reminding me she was proud of me. He told me the hairs on his neck were standing up. I wonder if he will ever come back.

Aging, a stealthy adversary

The next day, I couldn't move. Was it because of all the climbing around on the pergola? The worry of how we would pull this off in Covid times? The concern that the food wouldn't be right or no one would come? I don't think so. I think time had caught up with me. I'm finding I'm not as young as I used to be even though I am trying so hard to resist the passage of time. Much as I quip that we are all still three-year-olds in larger clothing, with all the same fears and insecurities, joys and potential to play, the body parts are definitely starting to wear. It's not so easy to get up off the floor anymore. When I get down there to play with my grandkids, they pop back up and go tearing off to do something else. Meanwhile, I remain on the floor trying to leverage my body back onto my feet.

Maybe it was because there had been a whirlwind of activity all summer long. During a visit with a long-time friend, we talked about mortality, how precious life is and the sudden realization that we have fewer years ahead than we have behind us. It was a sobering thought. And I still felt I was a youngster.

I noticed how many ads I had begun to receive. The ones for reduced cell phone prices and hearing aids that my ninety-something-year-old in-laws received. Included in the missives bombarding my inbox were "How to sleep better" and "How to boost your memory." This aging thing was beginning to seem real. However, as my hundred-and-six-year-old inherited friend Connie used to say, "What's the *alternity*?" I really don't know except to make every moment count. I was so flattered when, picking up my dog's food, the salesclerk asked if I qualified for the senior discount. Those moments are far more special than when the seventeen-year-old clerks assume I must be ancient and automatically give me the discount. It's nice to fool them some of the time.

My friends have said I keep far too busy and should be happy with only one activity a day. I still pack as much as I can into every waking moment. I figure if there is less time left, I better not waste any of it. I'm off to find something productive to do. As my parents used to say, "Don't just sit there. Do something." Maybe they were prescient and wished they had more time too.

Masking our senses ... if we have any to begin with

We were in year two of Covid and everyone for the most part was now adept at masking up. Though the extra effort was definitely a nuisance, I did have a good chuckle at the "Mask it or Casket" slogan I had recently seen. Protection for oneself and others made all kinds of sense. However, doing so was not without its challenges. Am I the only one who didn't see as well when my mask was on? Did anyone else find they did not hear as well? I certainly couldn't communicate as well.

You would think this mask business should have made all other senses sharper. But no, everything else was harder too. Either the mask rode up over my nose and into my eyes or I had to choose between breathing and seeing. If I breathed, my glasses fogged up. If I took off my glasses, I didn't see as well.

In addition to the constant reminder that all was not normal, masks muffled voices. It would take a speech language pathologist with a finely tuned ear to decipher what anyone was saying. Instead, I tried to find context to help determine what I was hearing, which turned out to be a wild guess at best. And when I spoke, I had to practically yell to be heard.

If one added a few years, the problem became more obvious.

What about the poor people like my ninety-eight-year-old aunt who had been deaf in one ear? She relied on reading lips, as do many seniors in their ninth and tenth decades of life.

Maybe I should have been more empathetic towards people who were hard of hearing or partially blind. I, for one, certainly wouldn't get behind the wheel of my car wearing a mask. The many sensory deficits would make that far too risky.

I heard that all through the pandemic eye makeup counters were quite busy, as eyes and eyebrows were the focus of much more attention. A genuine smile goes all the way to the eyes, but it was so hard to convey what you meant as a joke with just eyebrows and not a face-wide smile. I found myself saying, "That was a joke," just to be sure I didn't offend anyone with my sense of humour — about the only sense I felt was still intact after three years of the pandemic. Fortunately, humour has always been one thing that can be infectious without a health risk. Laughing was permitted too. We all needed a little more humour in our lives after those grim months. My mom always said, "Smile and the world smiles with you. Cry and you cry alone." There's probably something to that. She didn't invent the expression, she just lived by it.

Thinking back, what I really needed was a mask with a permanent smile on it. Then, no matter what I was thinking, people would have assumed I was happy and might have responded in kind.

There's a reason we have more than one friend

My mom used to say this. And now I believe her. You know how we always expect so much from our friends? When they let us down, they disappoint us. When they don't show up for a special occasion, we try to be gracious and acknowledge that our priorities are not always theirs, but gee whiz, couldn't they make an exception? When they begin a sentence with "You know I love you, but in this case you are wrong" and go on to take an opposing view to our own. I was talking with a friend the other day who said, "Ask someone else. If you ask ten people, you will get ten different types of advice." That's it! That's why we have more than one friend. There's an old story that says if you ask three rabbis you will get at least six different answers. Also, the more removed from your issue, the more objective the advice might be.

It's tempting to lean towards those who think like you do. It's much more comforting, to be sure. I notice that all of my friends are introverts on the Myers-Briggs personality profile. Interesting. I always thought I was more the extrovert type, but over time, I realize that may not be so. For my professional life I certainly had to be out there, and I learned how to make small talk very quickly. But as I get older, I am much happier sliding back into the introvert I was as a child. I remember spending a lot of time on my own and being fine with it. Since the pandemic curtailed most of our activities for so long, I don't miss getting together with friends and family. In fact, a lot of my friends are in their pj's by dinner time and abhor the thought of socializing on any large scale anymore.

The point my mom was making was that it is a lot of pressure to expect one person to be all things to meet all of our own personal needs. Having more than one friend means having more than one opinion. If you don't like one friend's opinion, you can always call another friend to see if they might agree with you.

Why must we live up to others' expectations?

What's wrong with our own expectations, just setting our own agenda and sticking to it? How is it that we let other people's thoughts and expectations derail our lives? Is it because we don't live in a vacuum? Is this how we live in a civil society, by actually caring about what others think, thereby taking our emotional intelligence and cues from them? Or is it simply because it was how we were raised?

The other day I was discussing this whole concept with my friend Sue. She was chastising me for putting everyone else first and doing what she said my mother would expect me to do. "Don't you realize how exhausting it is to be constantly doing for others?" she said. "Why don't you just stop caring what others think and let go of your mother's expectations? This is what she would do, but you don't have to. You are not auditioning for sainthood, after all. Besides, you are making the rest of us look bad." Ouch. That hit home. I don't really do anything to make others look bad. I just don't want to look bad myself.

Sue gave me a pretty powerful message. Maybe it is time I look after myself and stop worrying about ticking all the boxes. Have the kids for dinner. Check. Make sure my in-laws aren't alone on a Friday night. Check. Pick up a dress shirt for my husband for an upcoming wedding. Check. Visit my senior friends. Check and check. To be fair, I do set the bar pretty high for myself, but then I had excellent role models growing up.

It is that time of year when acknowledging everyone with a special gift is a tradition I carry on. But I feel myself coming down with the third cold in eight weeks. Is the universe trying to tell me something? Maybe enough is enough and I should knock it off before I run myself into the ground. Still, this is a very hard habit to break. It's not easy to put myself first and not feel guilty that I am letting someone down.

But then, do they really care, or is everyone too wrapped up in their own lives to notice that I have gone out of my way to offer some kindness? I suspect I put far too much emphasis on helping others, thinking it is the right thing to do.

And exactly who will be judging these good deeds? Will my aunt who can no longer remember a story she told me two minutes ago really notice if I visit this week or next? I think lightening my load is probably a good thing to do. This living up to others' expectations is a tough habit to break. Doing good in the world is one thing. Going to excess is unnecessary. I think I will spend the next few weeks focusing on myself for a change. If only I could be okay with that, I might actually enjoy it.

A true sense of accomplishment

We were hit by a sudden avalanche of snow last winter. About forty-five centimetres fell in a very short time and the city was crippled. Stay home, said the weather reports. Get off the roads, said the traffic reports. Too late. Optimists and those with what they thought were pressing commitments charged off, some without snow tires, and within hours the city was in a traffic snarl that led to roads being closed and drivers dead stopped for hours.

My husband realized that the snow on our driveway was already knee deep, so trying to get to the office was pointless. He had taken all of two days off for weather since he started his practice some forty-five years ago, one of which was this particular snowstorm day. Since my work was at my computer, no problem for me. The grandkids' first day back to school after the extended holiday would be spent playing in the snow if they could even get out of their house.

This was a massive snowfall. Pretty, but then we remembered the dog. She needed to go out, but the snow was over her head, and she is not a little dog. So, we got out the shovels and spent two hours cleaning off our back deck so she would have a place to go.

Walking her would be a whole other challenge, but we were sufficiently exhausted from clearing off almost two feet of snow that we took a break to assess. We live in a cul-de-sac that is always last to be plowed. We are not even considered a secondary road, and there is no access to a major thoroughfare, which is lovely and peaceful in most seasons, but we tend to be the forgotten ones in winter. No way we were getting plowed out any time soon.

I insisted that the dog needed her usual walk. What did she know of snow days? And so, with some convincing, my reluctant snow-shoveling partner joined me, in snow pants and high boots, warm jacket, hat and mitts to head out into the blizzard. We created a footpath so we could reach the street. So few cars had gone by that there were no tracks to follow. It was tough going, and before we had even reached the secondary road, we were soaking wet from the effort of climbing over snow and what the city calls "windrows," piles of snow the plows leave behind. The windrows had blocked off the roads at two entrances to our neighbourhood, and who knew when the plows were coming back?

The dog leapt over the snow with all the agility and grace of a training-school graduate. We, on the other hand, had to wade through the snow up to our thighs, sinking in and looking much less graceful as we struggled to maintain our balance. At last we reached a loop road that had been plowed and we walked on this, as the sidewalks had not been plowed. Normally, this would be unsafe, but the few drivers that had ventured out were now stuck, posing little threat to our progress. We weren't sure if the snow was more exhausting or the heavy winter gear and boots we were wearing.

About an hour later we returned home. I felt the benefits of having shoveled off our deck and yard for the dog and for braving our usual dog-walking route despite the snow. Though exhausting, it was also exhilarating, and I felt such a glow of accomplishment. I suddenly got a good idea of what my parents had tried to teach my sister and me all those years ago: it's not about achievement for achievement's sake, but feeling the satisfaction of accomplishing something we set our minds to, no matter how insignificant to the rest of the world. There were no accolades. No medal for participation or completion. No parade in our honour. Just the quiet satisfaction of not letting the weather keep us from doing what we needed to do. Wouldn't it be wonderful if that lesson could be taught in little league and children's soccer instead of rewarding team members for showing up?

I felt proud of myself for venturing out, and also for finally decoding the lesson my parents had wanted us to learn some fifty years ago.

Did the dog need a walk that badly? Probably not. I'm sure she could have figured out how to do her business in our own yard. On the other hand, guilt is such a powerful motivator. Wish those big brown eyes that can melt our hearts every time could melt some of that white stuff.

Two nights before Passover

We were having one last dinner before our house was totally turned over for Passover. Not everyone does this anymore, but my husband is a traditionalist. We were bringing out all the Passover pots and pans, dishes, glasses, serving pieces, a myriad of platters, wine goblets and other assorted paraphernalia particular to Jewish households at this time of year. Like others, we spent hours scouring the cupboards, cleaning, and replacing everyday food with those foods kosher for Passover. And we were hosting a Passover Seder on the first night of the holiday.

Three years had passed since we were all together in person at our table. Covid had done a number on us, making us wary of being together, so everyone in the family was going to test before committing to coming on the Friday night. Ah yes, a double whammy. Passover and the Sabbath on the same night.

I was trying to finish off cooking for the Seder. Our dinner was in the oven. I was supposed to be going online for a class and the telephone was ringing off the hook. The dog wanted her dinner and I wanted some peace and quiet. That's when a strange beeping started. Oh no! The oven computer was saying E2 F-3. I was thinking, I have my own malfunction code, which I am about to display. It's F U 2. The last time the oven flashed its E2 F-3 code, it locked dinner inside and cost us a new motherboard. Why in heaven's name did we need a motherboard and Wi-Fi as if we were going to call home and tell the oven to turn itself on? Honestly, technology has gotten out of hand.

Growing up, everything seemed so uncomplicated and sturdy. An oven lasted twenty years at least. I know ours did. There used to be a futuristic joke where a woman called home when she realized she'd forgotten to shut the oven off. The phone rang home and when it was finally picked up, the woman said, "Is this the oven?" And the voice on the other end replied, "Sorry, the oven is busy right now. This is the refrigerator, can I help you?"

It was no joke two days before Passover. I called my trusty appliance repairman and told him we had thirteen people coming for dinner in forty-eight hours. Help! He told me he would try to get a new sensor, but if that wasn't the problem it could be the motherboard, which no one is making anymore. We would need a new wall oven and the cost was outrageous. Our repairman drove clear across the city the day before Good Friday to secure this sensor for us.

In the middle of all this, my husband's administrative assistant was out with Covid and he asked if I could come into the office and cover for her. I dropped everything Passover related and tore down to his office to try to be of assistance. When the call came from my appliance guy that he had the part but was only available for the next half hour, I hopped back in my car and hightailed it for home. Bless him, he was sitting in our driveway when I got home. Fifteen minutes later and whatever magic he worked, we had an oven. I am so grateful for small favours. I was envisioning shuttling food by car from my friend down the street, as she too keeps kosher for Passover.

The other options were to cook using the stovetop, the microwave and the barbeque out back. Fortunately, my many pans and assorted menu items could all go into the oven after all. As I gratefully said to my repairman, "What is it with this holiday? Every year it is either the fridge, the freezer or the oven that goes on the fritz." He smiled and said, "You could always come to our Seder." I was dumbfounded. I figured he'd be celebrating Good Friday and Easter Sunday and that was why he couldn't come over on the weekend. Who knew he too was Jewish? And so sweet to invite us to their Passover Seder.

Rules and laws are for honest people

I don't know who coined this phrase, but I had cause to think about it the other day. I was struggling in the rain at a hospital parking lot gate trying to get the button to produce a ticket. No such luck. After a number of fruitless tries, I decided to just put my credit card in and, voila, the gate magically opened, just as an employee came running over asking if I needed help. "No thanks," I replied, "I just used my credit card, but thanks all the same."

Off I went to my appointment. When I returned to my car and drove out the exit, I realized I had not paid and that the gate was up. My first thought was "When is the gate going to come crashing down? When my car is right under it?" Then, "What if the machine thinks I never left and I get a credit card bill for staying there for many days?" And, of course, I realized before I went more than ten feet that the right thing to do would be to back up and put my credit card in again. Being an honest sort of citizen, I did just that and, lo and behold, after it took my credit card and told me I owed $8.50, a message popped up saying, "Surprise, it is your lucky day. No charge." Gee, maybe I should run out and buy a lottery ticket? However, I realized the gate to the exit was not just up, it was gone completely — broken. I guess the parking police had no alternative but to appear to be nice guys. Whatever the reason, I ruminated on the fact that I had at least gone back to do the right thing.

I was chatting with a friend about how many drivers cruise right through stop signs. "There's never a cop when you want one, right?" we agreed. And so many cars are seen hightailing it through our neighbourhood, which has a speed limit of forty kilometres. It's gotten bad enough that we have been offered Slow Down lawn signs from our city councillors. Seems we have become complacent in our nice quiet neighbourhood.

I was walking my dog one day when I saw our mailman on someone's doorstep. Yes, he is male; I hope I don't offend, but I refuse to say our mail person, or some other politically correct term. We still get mail delivery to super mailboxes, which have a community all their own on each street. But when it comes to parcels, Tom, our very kind and obliging mailman delivers to our doors. I have heard that there are porch pirates in every neighbourhood. Not in ours. Nope. Instead, they steal the mailman's van while the driver is putting a package on a doorstep and ringing the recipient's bell.

"Tom, why are you sitting there? Are you ill?" I asked. "And where's your van?" To which he replied, "They just stole it." Apparently, a truck pulled up behind his and, while Tom was taking a package to a doorstep not ten feet away, one guy got out, hopped into Tom's mail van and drove off. With Tom's keys and his wallet. In our neighbourhood. This was an eye opener.

Seems there had been a rash of car and truck thefts with people threatened at gunpoint. Fortunately, there was no gun this time, but Tom was clearly shaken. "Shall I sit with you 'til the police arrive?" I asked. "It's ok, they're on their way." And then three police cars pulled up. I said to the lead car's driver, "Please take care of our friend here. He is the best mailman we have ever had."

To this day, Tom has never gotten his van back. He had to buy a new one. He keeps his wallet and keys on a long retractable ring so where he goes, they go. Lesson learned. It's a hard way to learn it and disheartening when you realize that laws and rules are for honest people.

It's the age-old question. What would you do if you found fifty thousand dollars? Would you give it back? A group of us were discussing this over dinner. Someone bought a couch and when she removed the cushions, she found money. Should she give it back? It was a long discussion. Possibly the owner didn't know there had been money there. Perhaps it had been furniture from a long-deceased relative who had not believed in banks. Who couldn't use a small boost in cash? I can't remember what we agreed was the right response in the end.

And then there's something I learned at a huge chain grocery store. About fifteen of us were in the express lane, wondering why such a lineup. When I asked for the manager, he told us no one wanted to work. Not since the pandemic. When I got to the cash register the young woman staffing it apologized profusely for the wait. I told her it was not her fault. She was doing the best she could. She told us that what the manager said was not true. In fact, the staff all wanted more hours, but they were being cut by head office. Interesting. Where's the honesty and integrity in that?

I'll do it my own self! Three-year-olds have the right idea

When I was writing my first book, I was not even aware that I was starting something big. I thought I was just relaying some stories of my growing-up years. Imagine my surprise when, over the course of many months, I had created enough stories to compile a book. It was a heady time. The thought that I might actually be a writer, that someone other than my sister and I would be interested in what it was like being kids in this bygone era of the 1950s and '60s, was powerful stuff.

I wasn't sure the book was any good but I kept at it. Then I decided to go to a "self-publisher" to see what was what. The experience was frustrating, to put it politely.

From my very first phone call I felt like I was being handled. Every time I spoke to Jeff, my fast-talking customer service rep, I hung up feeling like we were living in two different worlds. I didn't understand anything he was telling me. At first, I deferred to him because when you don't know what you don't know, you think others have more experience and will surely want to help you. I did know that my brain just did not function at the light speed with which he spoke. I couldn't even keep up to take notes. I finally had to ask him to slow down.

After feeling my heart race during every conversation with him, I decided to practise my conflict resolution skills. I told the rep that I was feeling overwhelmed and I didn't think we were a good fit. Screwing up my courage, I actually asked to have someone else work with me.

Rep number two was lovely on the phone, kind and seemingly patient, talking very slowly (probably thought I was ancient and brain dead) until the fish was on the hook. There I dangled for days on end while hearing just how many months the process would take. I did not get the sense I was being guided through that process, but it sure involved many people, none of whom knew what the other was doing. I was sent lengthy documents with tiny print about which packages I could choose — in other words, how much I could spend.

I did speak with a number of publishing companies and looked up a few online. I figured I'd pick one and just jump right in. The problem was that they were not interested in teaching me what I needed to know. They just wanted to fit me into their process.

For $3,000 we do this, they said, and for $6,000 you get that and for the deluxe package (for my husband, deluxe means it is served with a slice of tomato), you get the works. For $15,000! They promised an initial review of the book, then an edit, but with no opportunity to meet with the editor or any of the suppliers who would be working on the project.

I never got to brief the illustrator, I was just told to fill out the forms. No, the designer would not read my book. "It's not our process," they said. But of course, they needed me to complete forms that basically gave a precis of each of the chapters so they wouldn't have to read them. A bizarre way to illustrate something about which they had no clue. Seemed I had to do more work just so they could do theirs. No, I did not want to rewrite a summary of the chapters where I wanted illustrations. In fact, I didn't think I wanted illustrations at all anymore.

It didn't help that somewhere along the line I lost my intended editor, who had been hand-picked for me by a writing colleague. The new editor the publisher chose for me wrote some excellent suggestions in the margins of my word document, but I was told track changes was as close as I would get to her unless I wanted to pay more.

I didn't take a package, but decided to pay as I went along, despite being told that was not economical. For whom? I was going to put a toe in the water until I got a sense of just how it all worked. Eventually, my "handler," as I had come to think of her, decided to give in and cover the cost of a phone call to the editor, who freelanced and was not on staff. Then came the back-and-forth through the author's portal on their website to schedule a meeting for the review. I would be allowed one hour in which to discuss no more than ten editor comments. I gave them my available dates and heard nothing back. By the time they sent some dates I was busy.

While caught up in their so-called process, I never quite understood who was doing what. What I did know was that I wanted a book with my name on it to be darn good. A year and a half later, I didn't feel any closer to having my book in print and out the door. To be fair, it was the middle of Covid and nothing was working the way it should, including this publishing process. There were paper shortages and staff shortages in the industry and who knows what all else behind the scenes.

Somewhere along the way I realized that my "handler" was sending my blood pressure through the roof. I decided this publishing firm was not for me.

I found a wonderful printer who, coincidentally, was from my hometown. He walked me through what I would need and when I would need it. He sent me a booklet on how to do this step by step and what they would help me with. Need to register the book? No problem. Need an editor? We will provide you with one. Need to figure out what size and how long my book would be? Here was the formula. Now, that was more like it. They had illustrators I could hire, someone who could design it and get the electronic version of the book out the door in seven to ten days. Within three weeks I could have as many print copies as I needed shipped to my door. I started getting into the process and doing much of it myself.

When it came to publicity, I did not want to have a fool for a client. Thus, I decided to get referrals to publicists who could do that part of the marketing for me. I was starting to feel much better about the book, looking forward to it finally being out. Maybe, as one friend told me, I was a control freak, but to me I felt this type of publishing to be a perfect example of being part of someone else's agenda. It was my book after all. I think the three-year-olds have it right. As many of them say at this age when over-eager parents want to help, "I do it my own self." I think I made the right decision.

Communication is a wonderful thing

I tell this to my husband all the time. Over the years I have discovered that communication is not his strong suit. I, on the other hand, am a professional communicator, with a good chunk of my life spent teaching others how to be clear and concise in their messaging, so I find it particularly galling when there is a communication chasm in my own home. My friends also have difficulty communicating with their spouses. Whether a friend and her husband are debating which sprinkler system to buy or deciding how they are going to spend the day, they are often not on the same page. One wants one thing and has no clue what the other has in mind.

Are all relationships like that? Are men and women really so different when it comes to communicating?

Just the other day, I went to call Elaine but I called my cousin Janet's home phone number by accident (I call Janet so often my fingers gravitated to her home number automatically). When Janet's husband, Brian, answered, I was surprised. Why was Brian answering the phone at my friend Elaine's?

Well, he wasn't. He was at his own home. I realized my mistake and carried on, asking about Brian's golf game and how he was enjoying the heat wave. Then I asked to speak to Janet, and he said she was out. I asked where she had gone and he said he had no idea.

Janet is always saying she never really knows where Brian is going when he goes out. He just never says. He's not really given to telling her anything — that her dinner was great or that he likes an outfit. Nice guy, but he just doesn't communicate much. So, when I asked him close to dinner time where Janet had gone, I was not being nosey. I just thought it odd that she was gone when she is usually home.

Being retired, they are part of that early bird set we all joke about, the ones who, by 4:30, are in line for dinner somewhere. These early birds are always joking about how late my husband and I eat, but for us it's a matter of necessity. My husband is still working at age seventy-two and won't retire for a few years yet. Once he does, I suspect we might not eat earlier, anyway.

Intent on solving the mystery, I called Janet on her cell phone. She answered right away, huffing and puffing. When I asked where she was, she said, "on my treadmill," which led me to ask, "In your basement?" "Where else would I be?" she replied. To which I responded, "Well, your husband doesn't think you are home. He told me you went out."

This surprised Janet less than it did me, but then she lives with him and his hearing is starting to go. Maybe he doesn't hear when she says she is going to do something. Maybe it just doesn't matter to him.

Then there is miscommunication during renovations. The tile guys assured me they knew the exact size to make the opening for the fireplace. The fireplace guy said, "Be sure to have them call me so I can give them the exact size." I passed the message on exactly as I received it. The tile guys thought they were good. Fireplace guy arrived this morning. Not so good. "How am I supposed to get the firebox in? There's no room for my hands!"

So, it isn't just wives and husbands who communicate differently. It is part of the human condition. Firebox guy insisted to Tile guy that he told me to make sure the space for the firebox was exactly the same as what we had before. First I'm hearing of it. When Firebox guy wasn't in the room, I told Tile guy I gave him the exact message I was given. And I have a vested interest: it's my house. He told me he didn't want to throw me under the bus, but I'm fine with being the bad guy. I'm the client. I am supposed to not know what I'm talking about and to keep changing my mind, and I chose to keep the peace. It got sorted out between the two of them. They both agreed that the book with the specifications was wrong.

As I always say, communication is a wonderful thing. We should try it sometime.

Communications age, indeed!

The other morning, I wanted to go walking with my beautiful next-generation Soft Coated Wheaten Terrier, Winnie, and I wanted my friend Connie to come along. Did I call her on the phone and say, "Good morning, how are you? Would you like to come for a walk with us?" Did I send her a quick email or text inviting her to come with us on our walk? No. I simply texted eight paw prints and a question mark. The funny thing was, she knew exactly what I was asking, as in previous weeks, months, years, and during Covid, I would send her a note saying, "Six paws are heading out for a walk. Want to join?"

Meeting up halfway between our houses, we started to chat while doing our best to avoid the huge piles of snow and slick black ice. I mentioned that I think we have indeed reverted back to the cave man and woman days. Here we are, with all the communications technology in the world, and what have we done? Created a whole generation and more of folk who can't "use their words." Technology has created short-form emojis for everything from feelings and thoughts to activity once left to the purview of the bathroom.

It is quite an eye opener. Between TikTok, Snapchat and Instagram, not to mention Facebook, now Meta, and Facetime and WhatsApp, it's amazing that anyone gets anything done. FOMO (fear of missing out) is rampant, ever more so among youth. With feelings and self-esteem being so fragile in the preteen years and on into adolescence and young adulthood, it is easy to see why no one wants to feel left out. And, oh, the damage that can be done when no one is paying attention to hurtful messaging! If I were in my school years I would not venture out of the house. Nevertheless, here we are. Is it any wonder that our attention is finally turning to mental health? How on earth are we ever going to have enough professionals to provide for all those who will undoubtedly need one?

My bigger concern is what has happened to communicating. As a professional communicator for all of my working life I knew exactly how to frame a situation, use messaging and key points, prepare someone for a media interview and alert the higher ups that an unaddressed issue was going to become a crisis. Today it seems everyone is messaging right left and centre. Even the media are basing their stories on Tweets from this one and messages from that one that may just be part of someone's agenda, with no basis in fact.

I worry where all this might end. Elections are fraught with potential hackings and falsehoods propagated by foreign infiltrators who are quite content to manipulate messaging to skew results. What happened to the good old days when our parents would say "Because I told you so" and we believed them?

What happened to media who travelled the world to where the action was and reported from the actual scene? Today someone in Montreal is reporting on events in Washington, D.C., and another reporter from London is filing a story on Ukraine. To me, all the news seems to be focused on the far left, tainted by said reporter's own biases, as if that view represents all of us. What, I wonder, will future archeologists or anthropologists three thousand years from now think of our twenty-first-century hieroglyphics?

That's my rant for the moment. It's no wonder I am so happily retired, especially from my former profession. Six paws are now going for a walk. Anyone want to join me?

Collateral benefits of renovation

What do hearing aids and a home renovation have in common? Not much. However, anyone who ever tried to do a home renovation, even a minor one, during the pandemic would wonder if anyone was listening. Lack of materials, supply-chain issues and scarcity of products like those you need for rebuilding a deck or installing wood flooring all played havoc with deadlines.

Our renovation was minor compared to the overhauling of some people's entire homes. For eighteen years I had been plotting and scheming to redo our den. Orange floor-to-ceiling fireplace, dated wallpaper, a raised hearth that was a huge concern when grandkids came to play (we envisioned split foreheads and other disasters, which had so far been avoided).

Yet, in spite of its shortcomings in style, the den was our favourite room in the house, with cozy couches and wall-to-wall books. From the day we moved in, I knew the den needed a major overhaul. However, the bathrooms needed upgrading due to black mold in the walls. Worn-out carpets vied for attention. A crack in the foundation needed an immediate remedy when we came home to find an unplanned indoor swimming pool in our basement.

Over time, the neon blue and purple bedroom colours chosen by the kids passed their best-before dates. Though the kids moved out years ago, they still used our basement as their personal storage space. Would anyone ever use the university textbooks again? It was not like they contained instructions for life. Posters and model cars, doodads, baseball caps and strange items of sentimental value were living rent free in our basement. With grandkids came all manner of highchairs, infant rockers, mobiles, riding toys, strollers and booster seats. We were well on our way to having our very own baby supply store. Boxes had gathered in our basement to the point that I had to call a halt to the storage. If you brought a box in, you'd better take one out. Sigh! I wanted my house back.

It was finally time for the floor-to-ceiling orange brick fireplace and raised hearth to go, the grass cloth of the '80s to be stripped and the fireplace (now a code violation) to be replaced. Never mind that my budget barely covered the cost of the wood flooring.

The renovation started smoothly. The fireplace became taupe and beige with blue highlights, with a mantle added, for more clutter. The walls were adorned with a lovely shade of taupe, or what our painter called "greige."

A few glitches due to specs from an old fireplace meant the tile workers had to come back. The new firebox had been installed with minor adjustments and we were finally ready for the flooring, which the supplier had loaded onto the back of someone else's truck, so it had to be reordered. When it was delivered a week late, it had to rest for two days in our home's humidity to be comfy enough so it wouldn't buckle. Too bad I didn't look at it right away, because it was not the right size or shade. Now it had to be exchanged. More delay. The delivery guys didn't really want to carry the new flooring in. Couldn't they just leave it on the floor inside the front door? Not if we wanted to walk anywhere in the house.

We were now two weeks behind schedule. This would not be so terrible if we did not have a wedding in three weeks, with out-of-town guests and entertainments in our home. Plus, there were hundreds if not thousands of books boxed up in our dining room, living room, bedrooms and basement vying for limited space with the kids' boxes.

Meanwhile, we looked at the foundation of our home through the disintegrating carpet of my husband's study and decided to replace that flooring too. We didn't think the room needed painting but when we took down all the pictures, we saw that the previous painter had left visible streaks everywhere. The problem became finding a painter, as ours was tied up for another few weeks with other jobs. We could not live with furniture in the middle of the room until he was free. Where to find another painter, a good one?

When we first moved into our home, Cousin Brian painted the entire place for us. Of course, now he was almost eighty. But still, this was just one room, so we asked if he would do this one small job for us, and he obliged. While discussing his availability over the phone, I asked in passing how he was managing on his own, with his wife away helping a friend put everything back in her newly renovated kitchen. He said he was fine, just off to get his hearing aids checked. (His wife insisted he hadn't heard a thing she'd said for years.)

On the day Brian came to our home, paint roller in hand, he handed me his old hearing aids. Seemed he was getting a new pair. I was thrilled, not because his wife's conversation would no longer fall on deaf ears but because, in passing, I had mentioned to her that my friend Tara desperately needed hearing aids and the price was exorbitant. My cousin repeated the story to her husband, Brian, and he graciously donated his old hearing aids to Tara. (Apparently, they can be reprogrammed.) What an unexpected gift. Not only did we get the study painted, but my friend Tara now had hearing aids. She was thrilled and I had been happy to help.

We had no idea when the flooring would actually be installed. The stacks of wood were still comfortable in our dining room. I was glad something was. We had no clue when we would be able to put our house back together. All entertaining would have to be done in the kitchen for the foreseeable future. It was the only room in the house without boxes.

Rising to the occasion

Our son was getting married and I had been under the weather for about three weeks. It was the virus from hell. Not Covid, mind you, although that immediately came to mind when the all-night coughing and the congestion in both head and chest refused to go away, even when threatened with antibiotics. Everyone dismissed it saying it was just a virus. And those were words no one took lightly at the time, as we were headed into yet another exploration of the Greek alphabet: Alpha, Beta, Delta,... Omicron. I was getting an education in a whole new language.

    I digress. This is about a wedding, which should have been a happy time, not one fraught with fears. Not, mind you, fears that our son was marrying the wrong woman or that this relationship would be doomed. Oh no. We were quite sure they were the love of each other's lives, especially since they had lived together for almost six years. As I said in our wedding speech, all those years he claimed to be staying with a university roommate, we had suspected otherwise. We were not as dumb as we pretended to be.

    About that speech: If you have been sick as a dog for weeks, no matter how hard you try to communicate with no voice, while wearing a mask, only interesting squeaks come out. Some messages cannot be conveyed with eyebrows alone, as we all know after two frustrating years of trying. Giving a speech at a wedding of a hundred and fifty in a mask was just not going to happen.

And about those Covid numbers: If you have been living together for six years, don't ya think you could pick another time to finally tie the knot?

And my, how weddings have changed since my first one some forty-five years ago. No trips to the printer for fancy invitations. Just a quick upload of your details and back story to a website and, voila, you have invited your guests with a minimum of fuss. As I told the kids, do put your energy into your marriage and not the wedding.

However, after being cooped up for longer than anyone cared to be, denied the simple pleasures of partying, these kids wanted a blow-out. The Covid numbers were coming down. The second vaccine was already working its protective magic in many of our friends and family. Did they have a Plan B? I didn't think so. Just lots of enthusiasm and naïve confidence that this wedding of one hundred and fifty would go ahead.

The day approached. The RSVPs were coming back. Not to us parents, mind you. No longer. We were just told where and when to show up and what the dress code would be. What a relief for us, and for them, when the Covid numbers continued to fall and it looked like the wedding would actually happen. I gathered my five pairs of shoes for the event — sneakers to arrive in, uncomfortable ones for pictures and getting down the aisle, sandals for standing for an hour of cocktails, another pair for dancing and, finally, flat ballet slippers if things got really crazy. Nothing worse than having your feet trounced on during a *hora* (traditional circle dance performed at all *simchas* — joyous occasions).

Photos were taken over many hours, pre-ceremony. The wedding documents, including the *ketubah* (a promissory note with Talmudic overtones given by the groom to the bride for her keeping), were signed. The female rabbi was delightful — there were none of those "when we were growing up" either — and we were ready for the service.

We were all down the aisle, and the ceremony went off without a hitch. Who even thought that in the middle of Covid, and indoors, this wedding would happen? I, for one, was hugely relieved. Now would come the fun part.

When our son showed us the agenda for the day, we noted he had left more time for the hora (forty-five minutes) than for the dinner (twenty-five minutes). Hmmm. We mentioned this to him but were told not to worry. This was correct. Little did we know what we were about to witness. Apparently, our son did get something out of twelve years of Jewish school. About forty-five lifelong friends! There they were, all gathered around the bride and groom, dancing like they had just been let out of captivity. Oh, I guess they had been.

I have been to many Jewish weddings and I can honestly say I had never seen anything like this before. From orthodox weddings where men only dance with men and women only with women behind a *mechitza* (dividing wall put up so men and women can party separately), to the more relaxed Reform weddings, this one was something to behold.

Our son was one of the last of his cohort to marry. He had waited a long time, both for his bride and for this special celebration. No wonder he wanted to enjoy every moment of it. Thing was, his buddies and he were all about fifteen years older than when they first started getting married, and probably not in such good shape.

Picture all of the young men grabbing both sides of a tablecloth and tossing the groom in the air as if on a trampoline. Then these same guys constructed pyramids with their bodies, one on top of the other and put the groom up on a serving tray to surf the room. I was on the verge of calling 911, heart in mouth and completely wonderstruck at the precision and skill these guys showed. No one got hurt, thankfully, and they seemed to have done this a time or two before, so well-rehearsed were they.

Perhaps one of the most touching moments of the evening was when my husband's then ninety-three-year-old mother got up to dance. When it was obvious her ninety-six-year-old husband could not navigate a walker on the dance floor, these same friends gathered round their table and danced all around the proud grandparents. It was a very special moment. Forty-five minutes of dancing and cavorting and tossing both bride and groom in the air, and putting us none-too-eager parents up on chairs as well. It all went by in a flash. I guess the itinerary was right on the money.

My only worry at this point was whether my voice would come out when I got up to the podium to help give the speech my husband and I had written. Fortunately, with my trusty tea thermos in hand and throat lozenge firmly in my cheek, I got through our remarks to laughter and some applause.

The bride and groom were so very happy and joyful. We were delighted for them. They said the wedding would happen and it had. (Would that we could all make things happen by wishing them so.) Denying Covid the opportunity to change their plans, they began their lives together in grand style. We had absolutely nothing to do with the planning or execution of what was pretty much a flawless wedding. I have to say, I was impressed.

Then Covid numbers went back up. Gathering with so many may not have been the best idea with such a sobering threat lurking around the corner, but I had to hand it to the kids. And in a way, we all felt a little better for having cheated Covid, forgetting about it even if only for a few hours. And no one got sick.

I was so grateful for so much, especially for the cold virus that had haunted me and many others for over a month finally going away. Maybe it was a message from on high to keep *shtum* (silent). After all, it was their wedding. Funny how time changes things. When we were getting married so many years ago, we didn't dare say anything. It was our parents who ran the show and made all the decisions. Nowadays it's the kids who run the show. We just show up. Once again, we missed our moment somewhere along the way.

Undercover spies

Every day there is a news item about protecting ourselves from unknowingly giving out private information. In fact, I was told by a young cousin of mine who had worked for Google, its parent company Alphabet, Apple and many other Silicon Valley biggies that we might as well get used to it. There is just no such thing as privacy anymore. Anyone can find out anything about anyone else in the blink of an eye. Now, there's a scary thought.

It is the information age after all, so it should not have surprised me that it's finally happened. My entire life is on the internet; well, at least my online retailer has gathered vast amounts of information about my person. Who knew this was going on? Not I. But then what did I think was behind all those tailored ads that come in when we are online? I have long suspected that, in spite of not owning a device directly connected to Siri or Alexa or anyone else out there in the stratosphere, all kinds of personal tidbits are being gathered as to our tastes in just about everything.

I'm sure that our private conversations are being recorded. Why else would I be talking about checking out Kelowna for a holiday and suddenly all kinds of ads with trips to British

Columbia are popping up on my iPad and other electronic devices? Undercover spies for sure.

While on the topic of undercover spies, I recently ordered a package of underwear online in my usual size and style. Thanks to Covid, I have gotten so used to this method of shopping. I no longer have any desire to set foot in a shopping mall.

When I placed the order, a notice popped up. It said in the politest, most discreet manner that "others who have ordered the same items you have ordered in the past have requested a larger size of this product." Really? Okay. Full marks for tact and diplomacy, but when I decide to order a specific size to literally cover my tush, I think I should know what size to order. How do they know I may have put on a few pounds? Are they also spying on my bathroom scale? Flabbergasted is an understatement in describing how I felt. You mean to tell me that now when I shop, I have to check with the online distributor to confirm my size? You are not my friend.

Underwear is rather personal and private, don't ya think? Well, I guess not anymore.

A very dear friend of mine wanted to order underwear from her favourite department store south of the border. She explained that she was reticent to do this because she was travelling with her kids and grandkids, who were also ordering items, and they were all having their orders delivered to their hotel room. My friend said she would be mortified if they accidentally opened up the package with her granny underwear. Some things are really personal.

And then there was the time my boyfriend and I were on a three-day trip to New York City. My mother asked if I would hunt down a certain kind of panty girdle that could only be found in the United States. Armed with her specifics and ready to launch my search on the lingerie floor of a large department store, I was about to wave goodbye to my boyfriend, who would surely go and sit in what we now call the husband chair.

No. We had been given an assignment and he was already looking through the racks of underwear without a shred of embarrassment. He was bound, bent and determined to find the exact size, colour and brand of panty girdle my mom had specified. I had to give him full marks. In fact, I decided such commitment made him worthy of marrying. Which I did. Of course, now he makes a bee line for the husband chair whenever we shop, and rightly so.

Back to the online intrusion of my privacy. I have no intention of marrying any online authority who has the audacity to suggest that I buy a size up in my undergarments. That is what I call chutzpah (audacity!). There was a board game with that title when I was growing up. I remember drawing one of the cards of chance as we moved dice around the board. It told me I had just received a shipment of two hundred and fifty brassieres and that if I cut them in half I would then have five hundred kipahs (skull caps/yarmelkes) with chin straps. My girlfriend and I thought that was hilarious and laughed ourselves silly. I do not find myself so amused any more. As they say, "He who laughs last, laughs best." The online retailer is probably laughing all the way to the bank.

The Top Shelf

Aging Is Not for Sissies

Lasting impressions

I went to see my ninety-eight-year-old aunt. She no longer remembers what she told me minutes ago. During one Covid visit, she kept repeating a story of when my mom moved to Toronto and didn't always know where she was going. My aunt would say, "Let me drive. You be the passenger." She had good reason for taking the wheel, being a good deal younger than my mom and a much more confident driver. And her services became a necessity once my mom no longer had a car after a mini stroke caused her to hit the gas instead of the brake and drive through a bank window.

Visiting with my aunt now, it was hard to remember how capable and competent she used to be. She did not attend university, but she was smart as a whip. She ran the fur department for a major high-end retailer in Winnipeg, then filled the same role in Toronto on Bloor Street. She worked for many years as a bookkeeper because, as she put it, in her day, young women did not go to university.

During another Covid visit, after we had all been vaccinated, I read her one of my stories in which she figured under another name to protect her innocence. It meant so much to me when she said "I'm so proud of you. Let me give you a big hug." With hugs in such short supply then, this felt doubly wonderful. I could hear the emotion in her voice when she continued, "I want to pick up the phone right now and call your mother and tell her how proud she would be of you."

My mom had been gone many years by then, and I was not sure what the telephone arrangements were with her location. Heaven Cell or Cloud Mobility? All I know is that my aunt's words felt so validating and reassuring. They had the power to warm my heart, a feeling I plan to keep forever.

The thing is, once parents are gone, they are gone forever. No more praise, even though we still long for it as grown-ups. Do we ever stop needing to be reminded how special we are? And who better than our parents to tell us?

I loved my aunt for sharing her enthusiasm with me. I loved that she had liked my stories. The best part was, I could read the same ones to her again and again because she did not remember them from one week to the next. No, wait, the best part was that praise she lavished on me. My heart remains warmed to this day.

The mystery of the QR code

"What's a QR code?" my husband asked. I told him I thought it was those squiggly unreadable lines inside a black box that had been popping up everywhere. If you want to check how old you are getting, just watch your grandchildren growing up. In the blink of an eye, they go from being tiny little babies to fully functioning, independent children. But I haven't aged at all, I think. Ha! Have you looked in the mirror lately? Have you been to the eye doctor? Is your hearing all that good? And then there is the QR code.

A year and a half into the pandemic, I went to visit a friend at a seniors' residence. My younger pals always teased me, telling me I should really get some younger friends to hang with. This one was ninety-eight, but I had another who just turned a hundred and four. How does one make such elderly friends? No, I don't volunteer there. I inherited them.

Let me explain. They were handed down to me by my mother, who has since passed on. For twelve years I had been lovingly checking in on her friends and, sadly, only three were left. Nevertheless, I visited them regularly, did errands as required and dropped off special little gifts to mark the Jewish holidays throughout the year.

That particular day was Rosh Hashanah, the beginning of the new year in the Hebrew calendar, so I was delivering goodies for a sweet new year, along with flowers. I was about to sign in at the front desk to comply with Covid regulations. I swear, you would think we were applying for fraternity or sorority membership — maybe Epsilon was coming and somewhere was a fraternity for cows called MU. I digress. As I was about to sign in, I was told to scan the QR code.

I was aware that such things existed, but I hadn't realized they had become such a mainstay of daily life that entry into a seniors' home required scanning it on my cell phone. Thankfully, a young person was on hand to point out that I needed to turn on this function through my settings to read the code.

Sure enough, I scanned the QR code and a whole new website popped up with the usual inquisition about any possible exposure. I'm pretty sure I had been nowhere in the past eighteen months, let alone the past few days. My existence at the time was home, garden, groceries, outside visit to friends, repeat. After answering the many questions on the website, prompted by the code I had scanned on my cell phone, I was finally admitted to the retirement residence. It's a sobering thought that when I was growing up there weren't any computers or cell phones, not to mention QR codes or bitcoin. Turned out QR stood for quick response.

My husband and I went to a Maroon 5 concert shortly thereafter. We were about 40 years older than everyone else there. The dance moves were different, the language was very different and the amount of alcohol and shots being tossed back was mind boggling. I decided I was quite happy putting a CD on our old CD player and listening to the music in my pajamas in our den.

Our son reminded us that our grandson, at age four, will find exactly what he wants to watch on the television using not only the remote for the cable, but also the second remote for the television and a third gizmo, a firestick. Where was he when we were trying to navigate a recent film festival and had to keep calling the support people to guide us through?

I'm willing to learn new technology. It just terrifies me. Apparently, our Smart TV is not so smart anymore. It's about six years old and requires a firestick and other important doohickeys to open up these new universes in which four-year-olds are quite competent. Our grandson's newest passion is outer space. I bought him pajamas with rockets and astronauts on them. Maybe I should get a pair for me in a larger size, because it's a whole new world out there. Technology is changing so fast I am constantly reminded that we are no longer the hip, "in" generation.

There I will be, in my space explorer pj's, happily listening to music on our old CD player in the den. No need to navigate the traffic to and from downtown. Just a few short steps from the concert to our bed.

Aging, the funny side

My mom lived to be ninety-something. We were never quite sure of her age as somewhere along the way her documents got lost in a fire. We think she fibbed about her age to make herself younger than my father when she married him. Maybe the deception began from the moment they met. In truth, my mom might have been a month or two older than my dad. No matter, once she made herself younger, she had to act it. Most of her friends thought they were older than she was. The point was, she never acted old. She had more energy than anyone I knew and perhaps I inherited some of it, along with her aging friends. I certainly never think of myself as old, just experienced.

My body has other ideas. I think it was in my doctor's office where I first saw a chart of how we look as children, then adolescence, young adulthood and middle age. The chart continued to older middle age, then later years, later senior years and finally old age. It was not a pretty picture. If the chart was accurate, and I'm on track with the diagrams, my body is definitely heading into its later years. But my mind doesn't agree. I was out looking for a dress to wear to a wedding when I found myself trying on bathing suits. Not that I planned to walk down the aisle at our son's wedding in a bathing suit, but I figured I was in the store already, and a bathing suit was a necessary evil if I ever wanted to go to the beach again.

There I was, in a very small change room on a very damp day taking off all of my clothing in order to stuff myself into a bathing suit. Did changing rooms get smaller or have I been expanding? This was one of the times I was thankful for gravity, counting on the earth's downward pull to help me launch myself into what surely must be the wrong size. If you've ever tried this exercise, especially during the pandemic, you will get my drift. I was glad I had chosen to go out of town for an anonymous day of trying on. Really, it was exhausting, more exercise than a complete workout.

The saleswoman was very helpful. She commented that the swimsuit I was looking at was for a bubby (Jewish grandmother). "But I *am* a bubby," I pronounced. "I have three grandchildren." Nevertheless, her point was well taken. Keep dressing young and you can fool some of the people some of the time.

Purchases in hand I headed home. On the radio the talk show host was discussing how to address those over a certain age. Were we Seniors? I kind of liked the term. It was respectful, had some dignity to it and allowed for special discounts because maybe we deserved them after all. Then the other talk show host opined that he thought Older Adult was a better term and heaven forfend, Elderly! Elderly? Now, that really rubbed me the wrong way. I never planned to be elderly.

My mother used to volunteer at a seniors' home in Toronto. At the age of eighty-six, she quit. Why? As she put it, the residents were too old. Okay, then. I guess I come by my dislike of "Elderly" and "Older Adult" genetically. The talk show host continued to say that he thought calling someone an elder was a sign of respect. I agreed. In the Indigenous community being a community elder is definitely an honour and a title of which to be proud. To me it sounded like someone who is expected to read scripture in church — someone who had been around for such a long time you wouldn't dare argue with them. No thank you.

I was quite happy when the pet store and the pharmacy announced special prices on senior day. That I can enjoy. In fact, last week, while I was hiding under my mask, a very young clerk asked me if I qualified for senior prices. I was so delighted that she thought I might be too young I wanted to blurt out, "Bless you, my child." Far better than the day ten years ago when the clerk at the drugstore automatically assumed I was a senior and gave me the discount without checking. I didn't know whether to laugh or cry.

Age is definitely all in one's head but lately it's been on my mind a lot. I'm still convinced I am a three-year-old in larger clothing, and if the bathing suit expedition was any indication, much larger clothing indeed. However, I still carry the same insecurities, fears and delights that I did when I was size 3. I'm not sure I want to spend my time worrying about who calls me what. I plan to retain my three-year-old attitude, finding joy and delight in all I can. I will leave the finer points of what to call my generation to those to whom it matters. I have more important things to do with my time, like going to play on the beach.

Either too young or too old

When I was eight or maybe nine years old, my parents, wanting to expose us to history, took us on a road trip to Washington, DC. I was thrilled with the hotel and its gift shop. In fact, I still remember a little spinning toy I purchased there. The statues of Roosevelt, Lincoln, Jefferson, the Washington Monument and the White House were of no interest whatsoever. What can I say? I wasn't being educated in an American school where students learned the Declaration of Independence and all of those other American statements of heritage and tradition. If I was not enthralled with American history (sorry, Mom), I was even less impressed with Canadian history. How one makes these things come to life for young folk I have no idea. I guess that's a line that divides good teachers and not so good ones.

On another trip, my parents took us to Ottawa to see the parliament buildings and other famous sites. Again, little interest on my part. On the long drive home, along with the inevitable "are we there yet?" I got car sick and threw up in the back seat just as we were approaching Kingston, Ontario. That in and of itself was not the main event. It was the guilt when my parents asked would I be willing to go see Old Fort Henry in Kingston, steeped in Canada's history of defending itself against the United States in the War of 1812. To me, that meant another stop, another delay in getting home. I didn't know Kingston was home to my dad's alma mater, Queen's University. I didn't really care to see where soldiers had defended our country in what seemed to me the Dark Ages. So, when they asked me to make the enormous decision of whether to go to Fort Henry or to head for home, I chose home.

Some sixty years later, my husband and I were going to Kingston for a weekend getaway. Part of our house was being renovated and it seemed like a good opportunity to escape the dust and noise for a few days. Of course, I thought of my parents and how disappointed they must have been so long ago when I had the chance to see Kingston and chose to go home. There they were, doing their best to impart important lessons, and I couldn't have cared less. Surely they were failing as parents. I never thought about it again until we saw the Kingston sign. I turned to my husband and said, "Maybe we should go see Old Fort Henry," and told him the story.

Our chief reason for taking this three-day getaway to Kingston was so we could play golf at a beautiful course. Once that was accomplished, we were free to choose any activities we wanted. We chose a bike tour of the city, visiting the university, the penitentiary, the downtown square, city hall and many sites along the waterfront. Our tour guide was a former Torontonian who fell in love with Kingston doing his MBA at Queens. We had loads of questions for him and he commented that we seemed so interested in history. Aha! I thought. At last, we would see Fort Henry. When I asked him if we could go there on our city tour, he replied, "Good gracious, no. That's a trip for much younger folk.

You would never be able to bike up that hill. We do that on the half-day picnic tour."

Hmm. As a child I was too young and now I'm too old? Maybe there is something to this carpe diem. Never mind. I thought I could make good with my parents, wherever they are now, but it was not to be. At least, not on this trip. Sorry, Mom and Dad. Next time we will drive there, I promise. So close, yet not meant to be. Three hours later we climbed off our rented bikes and headed back to Toronto. It was a great trip even though we didn't get to Old Fort Henry. I suppose if the fort has lasted over two hundred and fifty years, it will keep for another few. Maybe we will take our grandchildren there before they are too old.

Buried treasure

"Why are you out of breath?" my astute husband asked over the phone. Oh, I just carried my mom's clothing upstairs from the cedar closet. "Why have you kept her clothing so long?" he asked. Very good question. Why had I?

My mother had been gone for almost thirteen years. Her clothes could have had their own bat mitzvah this spring, based on the years they have spent in the closet. My husband's question was a fair one. "Oh, I don't know, I thought I might wear them someday."

My mother was tiny. A size 6 to my 12. In what world had I dreamt I might fit into her skirts and blazers? Maybe one arm would have fit! Nevertheless, I had been keeping them in a cedar closet — her cedar closet, in our basement — unable to part with them all those years. Sometimes I would go downstairs just to smell that distinct mom smell on her clothes. You know, the one you would always inhale during a brief hug. Little did I realize it wasn't my mom I had been inhaling, it was the cedar closet.

I heard that B'nai B'rith was having a clothing drive at a nearby shopping mall. I was getting rid of my own clothing, so it seemed like a good opportunity to finally detach a little from my mom's.

I was talking with a friend this afternoon. We were discussing what to do with our grandmothers' and mothers' good china — the pieces we only brought out for special occasions because they were rimmed with gold. It's not like our kids would want them either. Never mind the gold rims, if the china didn't go in the microwave or dishwasher, it would never suit today's lifestyle.

So, what to do with Limoges or Wedgewood sets, complete with underplated gravy boat and place settings for twelve? Where do they go for their next life? One could always plan dinner parties with fancy crystal and beautiful place settings. But, honestly, entertaining on that level has become a dying art that Covid helped kill off once and for all.

I did find a tea shop up north but they were only interested in the teapot. Figures. That was the one piece not in the set. Should I hunt it down just to sell the whole set intact? I think not. I tried another consignment shop even further north, again with no luck.

My friend and I wondered what the statute of limitations was on keeping heirlooms. And how could it be that they were not worth anything to anyone anymore? How sad.

I'm sure our mothers and grandmothers were looking down on us tsk-tsking from up there, saying, "Is nothing sacred anymore?" Those sets used to be so valuable. What happened to the next generations that they don't appreciate the fine art of hand-painted Limoges or carefully cultivated pieces of Wedgewood? My friend remembered how her dad would scrimp and save to buy her mom a new piece for her set on every birthday, Mother's Day and holiday. Accumulating the entire set must have taken years.

Now the only time my mother's china came out of the box was to be assessed for missing pieces with the worry that no one would buy the set with a missing gravy boat.

It's sad to think of how many civilized customs are going by the wayside. Our world has become faster for sure. Maybe it's not a kinder, more genteel world, but I had hoped to find a safe haven for those dishes. Perhaps an appreciative antique dealer might have the right clientele. Maybe even a museum. Surely, where our grandparents and parents are, they don't need sets of multi-piece dinnerware for lavish dining-room tables, nor do they require extensive wardrobes for all occasions. A bygone era, as they say. So sad to say goodbye.

P.S. I found a tea-shop owner who said he would take the china. He even came and picked it up. And in return? He gave me two five-dollar gift certificates for high tea. His generosity was overwhelming!

Goodbye Red River, gone but not forgotten

I grew up on a hot cereal called Red River. In our house this cereal was a mainstay. It was filled with all kinds of good grains and flax, and on Sundays this is what we woke up to. Hot Red River Cereal with cream and lots of brown sugar. Up until it was discontinued, we always had a box of Red River Cereal on hand. It was my go-to breakfast on Sundays and any time I couldn't figure out what else to eat. Sadly, my last box ran out. I went to numerous grocery stores only to be told they didn't have it. Fine then, I will call the company that made it.

Turned out it had been discontinued. NO! I told the customer service rep that this was not possible. That I had been eating this cereal for six decades. How could they banish something so wonderful from the grocery store shelves forever? I pleaded. I begged. I was reassured by a very soothing company rep that all our concerns and complaints would be heard. But how? By the little voice that always says my call may be monitored? I hoped so. I was truly incensed not to have been consulted before they did away with this focal point of my childhood Sundays.

I remember eating breakfast with my sister at her desk in her room so we wouldn't wake our parents. Sundays were their one day to sleep late. Didn't anyone at the company understand how healthy we had been all our lives? All due to Red River cereal, I was sure.

I made my pitch about how, with all the focus on healthy eating these days, Red River was surely the best thing ever invented. The customer service rep said I was not the only one who felt that way. Okay, then. Do something about it.

I hung up feeling that nothing I said would make a difference. I started my own marketing plan. Don't let Quaker Oats have all the success because they figured out how to package their product as Quick Quaker Oats. Why not make small packets of Red River? Just add hot water and stir. I began to think that the reason they pulled the item from the shelves was because not enough people in generations after mine were even aware of the product. It had never changed its packaging. Always the same red with the blue label across the circle on the front of the box. "Come on people," I thought. "Make this the instant cereal of choice. How hard could that be?"

I had no plans to go back into marketing at this point in my life, but I was hard pressed to find a way to get this product back on the market. If you have any ideas, do let me know — or better yet, let the company know. I want my Red River Cereal back.

Passing the torch *or* when will kids take on the holidays?

At what age do you acknowledge that maybe it's time to let go of all the responsibility for making a Seder or Rosh Hashanah dinner, or a Breaking the Fast or Chanukah party? Does this aha moment come at a specific point in time? Is it born out of absolute frustration and fatigue from having to do "all that work again"? Do offspring finally take the reins and say, "I'll do it"?

I can't remember when that moment came for me. I was in my early thirties when I awoke one day to realize that maybe it was time to offer to make a dinner for *Shabbat*, the Sabbath. Friday night Sabbath dinner is no small feat; it can be as elegant and complicated as a major banquet. In fact, in the Jewish faith, there is no more important holiday than the weekly Sabbath. And so, I took the torch, which had technically not been passed to me with any ceremony or acknowledgement. If I had suggested to my mom that it was time to let go of these entertainments in her apartment, she would have had a fit. No, I was more subtle and more aware of her feelings. While I wanted to know that if my efforts failed I could revert to her for all of the holidays, I had a niggling suspicion that, in fairness to my mom, my time to take over had come.

Not so today's youth, or at least those in our orbit. In fact, one of the kids asked if they needed to bring anything to a dinner I was hosting for the family. I responded with "Would you like to bring something?" Big mistake. His answer was, "Not really." Hmmm. I can't imagine accepting a dinner invitation today and showing up empty handed. When I was growing up it was a given that you not only offered to make something when invited to dinner, you also brought a gift for the host or hostess. At the very least you made a thank-you phone call or even sent a note the next day.

To be fair to the kids, though, I don't remember ever bringing something to my parents for dinner. It was always like going home and we were loved regardless. So, kids, even if you don't bring us anything for dinner, or offer to, we still love you. Still, while civility may be a dying art and thank-you notes have gone the way of the dodo bird, how 'bout a quick text or a Facebook message for your host?

Speaking of dinners, they don't make themselves. I put so much effort into mine that one friend is afraid to say yes when she is invited. She immediately gets concerned that, because she doesn't prepare to the degree I do, I won't be pleased to get her invite, or I will somehow be disappointed. In fact, I am delighted to not have to worry about what to make for dinner, or to prepare it and clean up after. A night off? Marvelous. Order in for all I care. Just get me out of my kitchen. Please.

This Friday night is just a regular Friday night and my friend and her husband have agreed to come. Nothing fancy. Some chicken soup and chopped liver. Roast chicken and leftover potato latkes (pancakes). Maybe a veggie, if they are lucky. Just come have dinner with us and keep us company. Of course, my friend offered to make something. I guess it is our generation. I think young folk today are quite happy to invite friends over and order in, sharing the cost. I don't see much of that battling over the bill we grew up with.

Now that three of the offspring are married with their own homes, I'm still waiting for the day when we get an invitation for Shabbat dinner or one of them steps up to the plate and says, "We'll host Rosh Hashanah this year." The best excuse so far for not inviting us is because "our place is too small." Too small? Do they have any idea how our parents lived when we were kids? I remember having a den that sat six and there were twenty-three of us gathered on the floor, on the chairs and leaning against the walls and each other. Who needed space? That was no excuse not to have people over. In fact, the smaller the space, the greater the challenge — a kind of how-many-friends-can-we-fit-in-the-phone-booth kind of thinking.

Much as I would love to pass the torch, I suspect there is no one running a close second behind me, ready to take the handoff. Maybe I need to be less subtle and announce that this year is my last Passover Seder. "We are now going to take turns. Who's first?" I can just imagine the silence that will follow. Oh well. For now, I guess it will be our turn yet again. I think I am going on about thirty-five years and still counting. At least I know where we can hide the *afikomen* (the middle matzoh that the youngest is supposed to find during the Passover Seder and trade for a gift) and I might even remember where the Chanukah decorations are. Letting go of making all the holidays may not be as easy as I would like, but I'm certainly ready when they are.

P.S. Be still my beating heart. Just as this book was going to print, son number three announced he is hosting Rosh Hashanah dinner this year. Mazel tov!

The perfect birthday present

When our grandson turned five, we thought it would be fun to let him pick out his own present. We set a date and arranged to pick up the little guy. Car seat installed we were all ready to go to the toy store. Delight showed all over his little face as we started on our journey. No younger sibling along, he had us all to himself, as we had him.

Upon arriving at the toy store where all manner of games and creatures and stuffies and vehicles awaited, he promptly took off to the action figures, where he oohed and aahed over figurines totally foreign to us boomers. Look Zadie, there's Tattoo Man and there's Vulcan. "Who's this?" we asked, pointing to a somewhat scary and multi-muscled hulk of a figurine. "That's The Hulk" he exclaimed without even pausing. Seems our grandson's world was a completely foreign universe to the one we lived in. "This one?" "Oh, he's a bad guy." "This one?" "He's a good guy." Okay, then. The forces of good and evil still exist. They just look a whole lot creepier than anything we recognized. Seems the creepier the better.

Next it was off to the dinosaurs. What little five-year-old can resist? It wasn't long before we reminded our little shopper that we were there to pick one gift, so how 'bout we get a cart and start putting in possibilities. There were lots of action figures, including one Captain America figurine he was clutching tightly. By the time we had investigated all manner of scooters and electronic toys, including ones that talked and others that just hulked silently, waiting for youngsters to give them a voice, we were exhausted. Our grandson, however, still had loads of energy.

We eventually worked our way through the items gathered in the cart to decide which ones were priority. We decided to save a dinosaur for Chanukah a few short days away, and for his birthday he chose a very inexpensive figurine, the Marvel character he had been holding all along. Seems they had already become friends, discussing the pros and cons of each toy he was considering. I guess that happens when you have been an only child for three of your five years and parents allow you quiet time to explore your imagination.

We decided that picking up a book for his younger sibling might be a generous idea. He was getting the birthday present, but it was nice to acknowledge that his sister might feel a wee bit left out. We also felt we were getting off lightly, with an inexpensive adventure figure, so we added an electronic learning tool with an outer space theme for good measure.

We spent another hour together going for lunch where all kids his age love to go, and then it was time to return home. He was thrilled to show off his new toy to his dad and mom. We reminded him about "his" little gift for his sister, but he quickly announced that it was not from him but from us. I guess age five might be a little young to care that his little sister would not be getting a birthday gift. Off he ran to continue his conversation with Captain What's His Name.

It's a whole new world out there. The Yogi Bears and Quick Draw McGraw's and Oggy Doggy and Doggy Daddy, along with the Huckleberry Hounds of the past, are well and truly from another generation. We will just have to get with today's program: Peppa Pig, Baby Shark, the characters from Frozen, Encanto princesses and a whole slew of dinosaurs and Spiderman characters. It's so hard to keep up. I'm sure our grandchildren think we are the dinosaurs. I bet they can teach us a thing or two.

Oh goodie, a brand-new fire-engine-red ... Rollator!

Every senior's dream? I'm not sure. But oh, the excitement when this is one's only opportunity to get out there and get moving. It doesn't have the same ring of enthusiasm that getting a first tricycle or, better yet, a first two-wheeler had. Now it's a four-wheeler. Yippee.

If you have ever tried to get your elderly relative to embrace the freedom and safety of a four-wheeler, better known as a walker, as I have, you will know it is not looked upon with the same anticipation and glee as their first modes of transportation. Even a little red wagon was more exciting. It was the beginning of freedom to go out and see the world.

Sadly, as my mom aged, she dreaded even the thought of needing a walker to get around. Rather than seeing it as a way of having a bit more freedom, she viewed needing a walker as practically a death sentence and dreaded its arrival.

Getting my mom to agree to use a cane was a major ordeal and she lost her balance a lot. She was in too much of a hurry to be slowed down by a cane. Then came time for a walker. No way. First, after a hospital stay with a broken limb, it was one of those lightweight metal walkers that need tennis balls indoors so as not to scratch the floors. I remember slicing into a perfectly good tennis ball or two for my husband's walker when he had his hip surgery. Fortunately for him, it was the hip that would be permanent, not the walker.

My friend Paula told me a story about a book she read in which the next generation came to a resort in the Catskills where the family used to spend the summer. What happened to all the tennis balls? Apparently resort staff had to hide them, as seniors were stealing them for their walkers. Times change. Life moves on. The plethora of tennis balls that used to excite us as children learning the game serves a new purpose in our geriatric years. "Oh, look at all the tennis balls. Let's take two for our walkers so we can get around better."

Having inherited my mom's senior friends after she passed, I got to spend a lot of time with this older generation and came to learn about their worries and fears, which went beyond life's usual challenges. Thoughts about aging often kept them up at night, especially the fear of losing control. How hard they had worked to master all those skills in childhood — learning to walk, rolling down a hill like a sausage, jumping in the leaves and the snow, learning to ride a bike. Over a lifetime of challenge and success they mastered many skills, became competent and confident. Those were the best years. The ones where no one had to think before doing. Fast forward into their later years and along came the fear of falling and breaking something — and beyond that, the fear they wouldn't be remembered in the best light (though that is another story).

From the time we are born, we all put so much energy and effort into moving toward independence with speed. Is it any wonder that older seniors fight with just as much vigor to hold onto that independence by hanging on to their driver's license, retaining the ability to get around on two feet and continuing to do the things they struggled so hard to learn at the beginning of their lives? Is it any wonder they resist dependence with so much effort?

For now, I'm just grateful to be able to get around on my own two feet and push the thought of a walker as far ahead as possible.

We can't take ourselves too seriously *or* get out the scissors

That cannot be me. Am I that old? How many of us look at a photo captured at an event and immediately zero in on all our visible flaws. Such was my recent experience when looking at the pictures from our son's wedding. Who is that old, flabby woman? Oh my God! It's me. It's a frightening prospect when I look at myself through a photographer's lens. What was he thinking? What was I thinking? That dress is not flattering at all. My face has aged and it is sagging in places I didn't even know there were places! Is that my jaw? Why are there potholes in my cheeks? Are those dimples? Can't be. Is my face collapsing? Why do I look twice my size? Or, as my mom would say when looking at a picture of herself as she aged, "Where are my scissors?"

There are two definite ways to determine that we are, in fact, aging, like it or not. One, we can look at our grandchildren or our friends' grandchildren and see how quickly they are growing. The other is to see ourselves in other people's photographs.

My mom had a foolproof way of dealing with any picture she thought unflattering. She would simply get out the scissors and cut herself out.

The photographer our kids hired for their wedding was so patient and caring and captured the bride and groom in the most flattering light. (But then, if you don't look amazing on your wedding day, when do you?) They were all aglow, confident in their decision that they had chosen their special mate, hopefully for life. But honestly, their feet weren't killing them, and their bodies weren't screaming to be let out of the captivity of control-top hose. They didn't have to choose a gown or dress that hides a multitude of sins.

Included in the photographer's checklist must be "don't embarrass the bureau." In plain language, do not make the mother of the bride or groom get out the scissors. Those of us who played supporting roles (and I don't mean the pantyhose I would put my toe through before the evening was out) were not the focus of the event; therefore, from the photographer's point of view, who cared what we looked like?

Well, I did. I didn't want to go down in posterity with all my flaws on full display for generations to come. Not that future generations would care, I am sure.

I often wonder what other family members do with all their parents' photos. My husband carefully goes through thousands of photos from his parents' trips all over the world, pausing to look at people he doesn't even know, trying to decide what to keep and what to toss. Oh, the guilt that goes with tossing those photos. If I could be sure those of me at this wedding would never see the light of day or that they would get tossed out with the garbage, I wouldn't feel so bad. But what if someone actually sees me like this?

In her generation, my mom could look at a photo, decide she looked awful and cut herself out. Today we live in an electronic age where it is harder to ensure your photos are removed because they are now digital and someone else has the master copies.

More loss of control. Aging is tough.

Photos can strike fear into the heart. I have a friend who insists she never takes a good picture. She just slinks off and hides behind someone else when the cameras come out. Sadly, I fear that I too will be doing that shortly.

Unflattering pictures aside, and scissors at the ready notwithstanding, I do believe it is what's on the inside that matters most. On the inside we still just want to belong and be loved. On the outside we are just more grown up ... more experienced, with an added wrinkle or two here and there.

The bride and groom looked positively beautiful. I hoped everyone was focused on them. At the time I remember musing, when the evening ended, "How fast can I get my pantyhose off?" Looking back, I should have just burned them.

It's about those shoes

At a recent wedding, I was struck by just how high a heel young folk wear to formal occasions. Stilettos at least four inches high, with pencil-sharpened toes. Anyone my age certainly can't navigate the world on such tiny heels. They might be good for aerating one's lawn, but how on earth do these fashion mavens stand in them all night and even dance in them, confident they are not going to slip and fall? (Though, I guess slipping and falling is more a preoccupation of my generation and older.) My littlest toes would not fit into these contraptions worn by all the under forties at this affair. It's too much of a death-defying act — though I could certainly use the height.

Speaking of heels, mine on my trusty dog-walking snow boots are totally worn down to the point where there are holes in them. Yes, I have boots just for walking our pooch; in fact, I have an entire wardrobe for that purpose. Don't tell my mother. Thankfully, dogs don't judge. It had been so long since I visited the shoemaker (fondly referred to by said mom as the cobbler) that I had no idea where to go. My mom had a wonderful Russian shoe repairman stationed in a central shopping centre with outdoor access. His very tiny shop had two chairs to sit in while you waited as he honed his craft on your shoes. He smoked like a chimney so you were taking your life in your hands going in there, but he was very, very good and very affordable. New heels? Ten dollars. You need them today? No problem, have a seat.

Sadly, the site where this shop existed for more than forty years is now a huge condo. Our cobbler knew this was coming and got ahead of the curve by moving a few blocks north to where a brand-new condo with two towers had already opened. There was outdoor access, but no parking, so no way to just run in to drop off or pick up your shoes. As business dwindled, he moved ninety minutes further north to a new city altogether. Much as I liked his work I was not going out of town to get my heels fixed.

I decided to try a cobbler closer to home. He had good reviews on social media. It would be an adventure. He too was located in a new condo tower, but this one with outdoor parking just behind the building, and outdoor access too. So off I went. Lo and behold, what did I find but another heavy smoker tucked away in an even smaller space that also provided dry cleaning, key cutting, and all manner of other repairs in addition to shoes. I left my boots wondering if I should have asked the cost. But the price was irrelevant. There were holes in the heels and my dog needed her walks.

The next day, as promised, shoe repair guy called to tell me my boots were ready. That will be thirty dollars, please. Really? What happened to ten dollars? Have I been sleeping for so long that the price has tripled? Maybe I have been under a rock all these months? Maybe Covid had been so insidious I needed to get out more.

We hear about the cost of dry goods going up along with the rising cost of beef. But thirty dollars for a pair of heels? To be fair, he did a really good job and also polished my boots, and I did need them repaired. But would he charge that for a mere sliver of a heel, the kind that goes on a four-and-a-half-inch stiletto? Or do those shoes get worn so rarely they never need new heels? The truth comes out at last. I suspect that no one wears them often because they're killing not only feet, but backs and balance as well. Not to mention the threat of getting caught in a heating grate on the sidewalk.

Never mind. My boots were repaired. I had new heels. It was worth it just to see my dog's face light up as we headed off for our third walk of the day.

Aging gracefully

The thing about aging is that the experience is as unique to each individual as are all of our quirks, habits and foibles. No two people age alike. I was discussing this with my husband the other day. He told me that the onset of the old age progression can begin at any point after you enter your sixty-fifth year. For some it happens earlier. There is no predicting when it will arrive. If you have good genes (I do on one side of the family and he does on both sides), then your chances of living longer are better. On the other hand, I have friends who have outlived their parents by ten to twenty-five years already.

My husband did point out that once the aging process sets in, it is a steady progression (downhill, I presume, although he did not say that). While we age at different rates, some people are genetically predisposed to age during young old age (sixty-five to seventy-five) or during middle old age (seventy-five to eighty-five) or during old, old, age (eighty-five plus).

Apart from the quite often hilarious aspects of aging, different folks approach their eventual demise with a variety of responses. Some, like me, choose to look at the lighter side and laugh about the situation. Others have a sense of impending gloom and doom. There are those who get the funeral home notices sent to their email every day. I've heard of planning ahead, and certainly the funeral homes like it when we do, but how is that uplifting or setting us up for a positive mindset as we start our day? I understand looking at the obituaries in the newspaper and going online to get more details when you know someone has passed away. But having notifications of who dies sent to your email on a daily basis? As my husband likes to joke, if you check the obituary page in the morning and your name isn't there, it's a good day!

I once asked my mom (who lived to be ninety-something) why she always had the sports section of the paper open. My mother was no athlete and had absolutely no interest in any sport that I knew of, yet there was that section on her dining room table. Turns out the obituaries were on the back page of the sports section and that page she was very interested in.

Now in their nineties, my in-laws have outlived many of their friends. I understand if they are interested in their declining ranks, but I don't understand a sixty-something-year-old being obsessed with who died today.

Then there are those who have organ recitals on a regular basis. And I don't mean the kind where you set forth onto the stage where proud parents and friends await to cheer your performance. No, I'm referring to the one where seniors get together and recount all their ailments. Oh, my hip! My back is killing me. My aching bones and cracking knees. Oy. Oy. Oy. In fact, there are many seniors who spend most of their time enumerating their aches and pains, constantly regaling their friends with a litany of ailments and complaints of body parts that no longer function properly.

I think the less one thinks about aging, the better for one's mindset. Maybe my mom had the right idea in fibbing about her age so she would not be the older woman by six measly months. My dad never knew. No one ever found out. To this day, we don't know what her exact age was, but possibly she believed, as I do, that we are only as old as we think we are. Some famous philosopher said we are what we think, so we must think young. We must think healthy. We must think fit! And let's not divulge to anyone who doesn't already know that getting up off the floor requires a whole new level of effort in moaning and groaning. So does getting out of bed, putting on our boots, getting into and out of a heavy winter coat and, above all, bending down to pick up presents from our dogs. Why don't more seniors have dogs? It's not that hard to bend down to pick up after them. But it is so hard to get back up.

These, I think, are the true secrets of aging gracefully: don't talk, don't tell.

The graying of Canada

It's the old question women of a certain age face sooner or later: To colour or not to colour? One's hair that is. (Although there is also a huge variety of colouring books for adults now, meant to relieve stress while requiring less creativity than doodling.)

After two years of on-again, off-again lockdowns, my hairdresser was certainly missing many of her clients. It hadn't dawned on me until a recent visit, when we were discussing my own locks, that her business took a huge hit, as did many during the past two years. I learned she was only working three days a week, which was why getting an appointment was so difficult. I also learned about the constant struggle in the salon where she worked to get staff and clients to wear their masks, and to wear them properly. You don't know what others' troubles are 'til you ask.

My mother always taught me that as you get older you should lighten your hair. She didn't mean that everyone needed to go blonde, but if you are dark haired, as am I, it is much easier to hide the gray when your original colour is a lighter one. I have had a constant battle with my hairdresser to keep my hair a mid to light brown. At a certain point, I decided I did not want to look like a madam in a brothel, but rather wanted to age in a less noticeable way. Never mind the double chin, the sagging eyes, the deepening crevices from either laughing too much or not enough.

Her opinion differed. "Your hair gets bleached by the sun too much. Orange is really not a good look." Try as I might to convince her to go to a light brown, I always left the salon with much darker hair. Last visit I actually read her the riot act. I said jokingly that I wanted to find a light brown that looked good on me, or I might just decide to let the gray come in permanently. Her response was equally joking. "Are you threatening me?" I think I was. After all, it is my hair.

Most of my friends gave up on colouring their hair long ago, and I admit that, on them, the gray looks fine. But the thought of being gray and perhaps finally acknowledging my true age gives me pause. One of my "blonde" friends decided to go gray naturally years ago. She started by having her hairstylist do a gray rinse so she could see how it looked. Next time I saw her, her hair was blue. Oh no. A friend younger than I had become a member of the blue-haired set. The next time we met her hair was purple. She was having fun deciding what colour her hair should be. Would that I were brave enough to even contemplate that idea. No way.

On the other hand, having gray hair does lend a certain gravitas and experience to any opinions one might share. Even the queen of England went gray at some point. It all depends on whether the aging of Canada is seen as a good thing or a bad thing. We baby boomers have certainly been the majority of the population for a long time. We tend to look at the generations following us the way all older generations have before us: We are the ones who know what is best. We have earned the respect our experience would suggest. On the other hand, we have done a pretty good job of creating offspring who not only think they know best but are entitled to know best. And maybe they do.

All this is far too complicated for me. I just want to know if and when I should let my true colours out. Not yet, though. Maybe when I am in my mid-seventies. That way I can put the decision off for a few more years. In the meantime, any urge I have to colour anything will be confined to those new-fangled, anxiety-reducing, decision-delaying colouring books.

The doctor's appointment

Going for one's annual physical should not be a traumatic event. I for one have not been for a physical in recent history. This is not because I have anything against doctors. I married one. I was the daughter of one. I think participating in one's health is a requirement of living. And I do all the normal proactive things like exercising, trying to eat well, watching my cholesterol, buying low-fat foods and trying to stay away from ice cream and foods with high sugar content. Note that I say "trying." Also note there is no mention of chocolate, as I am a confirmed addict of all things chocolate. However, I do "try" to eat properly.

I used to chuckle when I heard about seniors going to dinner at 4:30 or 5:00 p.m. for the early bird specials. In fact, I thought that was hysterical and would often kid my friends who ate early. That's not really an option in a doctor's household. As a child I learned to wolf down dinner at almost seven in the evening, trying to keep up with my dad who would then go off to check on patients at two hospitals, and *then* make house calls. I know. Pretty much unheard of today.

Today my husband comes in between six and nine, depending on the day, meetings and his late night at the office. Dinner is never on the table before seven o'clock and usually we are still at the table closer to eight o'clock, he taking his time eating all the things on his plate in equal amounts and probably in a specific order so he finishes the last bite of everything at the same time, and me with a long since empty plate. Old habits die hard.

I now understand why seniors want to eat early. My first attack of acid reflux, also known as GERD, or severe pain in the esophagus, came about a year ago. As anyone who has had it will tell you, such pain can resemble that of a heart attack and scare you half to death. Eating with GERD becomes a question of what to eat at which time of the day so you don't lie awake all night mentally rewriting your will. I get it now. Going to bed on a full stomach can mean sitting upright all night just to avoid said acid reflux, where dinner decides it is coming back for a late-night visit.

Back to the annual physical. We had just been away for two weeks, eating all our meals in restaurants. It's true what they say about salt in restaurant foods. As the kids say, it is "ridiculous" how much salt is added to the meal before it reaches your table. And no one is measuring the oils or fats used to prepare your dinner; they just want to make it taste good so you keep coming back. I don't think they intend for the meal to keep coming back, though, and it is never as good as the first time.

It was with trepidation that I agreed to an appointment two days after returning from holidays. As I got on the scale per the nurse's request, I was still wearing clothes, making the verdict even worse. In what mind was I when I thought coming to the doctor after two weeks of eating on holiday was a good idea? Never again. "Can I take my clothes off at least?" I asked. "No, you can't do that here." "I will if you will," I countered. "You may take your boots off," the nurse replied. First, my weight was higher than it has ever been. Then, the nurse measured my height and proclaimed I was two inches shorter. Oh wonderful. If I keep eating, I will be a perfect square! Before I even mentioned the next part to a friend, she asked if they brought out the dreaded tape measure, saying how she hated that most of all. Indeed, to add insult to injury, a tape measure was brought out to assess my waist. What is that for, I wonder? To see if the two inches I lost in height had moved to my middle? Probably.

With all the good news I had just received, the nurse proceeded to announce she was now going to take my blood pressure. Was it any wonder my blood pressure was through the roof? They really know how to make you feel good, these health care workers.

In contrast, the actual physical was fine, with the doctor noting I was in good shape. "Have you ever been scoped?" she asked. "No, and I have no intention of starting now." I can explain the acid reflux. I had an emergency piece of chocolate cake before bed. I won't be doing that again. Gone are the days when I can indulge in treats late in the day.

My doctor did fill some prescriptions for me, one for physio, another for orthotics, and the usual medication. Then she suggested I take my blood pressure for two weeks every day at different times to make sure it was coming down. I did and it is.

I think the world of my doctor. She is bright, astute and very caring. She also teaches at the faculty of medicine at a university and has just won a teaching award. When I do go to see her, I feel she is a kindred spirit, and we don't see each other very often, which is also a good thing for the right reasons. However, there is still the scale, and the shrinking height and, *chas v'chalilah* ("heaven forbid," as my mother would say), the dreaded tape measure. My mother also used to say, "Getting old is not for sissies." I now know what she meant. Time marches on. I no longer laugh at the early-birders. I see myself joining them in short order. Two inches shorter, to be precise.

The leopard never changes its spots, unless you ask nicely

My husband is very sweet and for a recent Valentine's Day he came up with the right gift. What could go wrong? Roses are always a big hit with me and every year he brings me a dozen beautiful red roses. We go out for dinner to celebrate the evening and exchange loving cards. All good. That is, until we get to the bag he hides under the table, which I open after dinner.

How do you tell your thoughtful husband that the little negligee — and I do mean little, no more than three pieces of dental floss — is really not your thing? I have tried in the past to tell him tactfully that the chances of me wearing such things are slim to none. For a number of years, I discreetly got rid of these gifts (thankfully, he never asked where they went, and they are not the kind of thing you can donate to the charity boxes). Finally, I just came right out and said, "I will gladly wear these when you do." Do men have any idea how uncomfortable that stuff is? That put an end to the giving of lingerie. I pointed out that if he wanted to give me something I might wear, pajamas were a better idea.

So now, every Valentine's Day I get a new pair of pajamas. Not just any pajamas, but ones that have significant meaning to me. Some years there have been pj's with dogs. This year was the year of the leopard, or perhaps it was a cougar, although my husband is older than me by two years so that couldn't be it. Or maybe it was a cheetah print. When I opened the gift, I noticed it was a size small petite. Okay, maybe one arm would fit. I haven't been a size small petite since I was about ten years old. Nevertheless, it was a lovely gift and he gets an A for great effort.

I suggested we exchange it for a larger size and contacted our favourite online purveyor of all things consumer, who said yes, they would take it back, no problem. My husband in his haste to make things right clicked a larger size. However, what arrived in the next shipment was fleece. Poor guy. I explained that I am far too hot at night to wear fleece, ever, so back the pajamas went. By this time, I was getting to know the company staff far too well. I dutifully filled in all the forms to send the gift back. Finally, my husband assured me he had ordered the right size in one hundred percent cotton. Unfortunately, a few days later arrived a medium top and a large bottom. Okay, then. What has happened to quality control? And why, when I had asked if I could get the top in large and the bottoms in medium, was I told no mixing and matching? Oh well.

The medium top fits perfectly. The bottoms? They are going in the hot cycle of the wash and dryer, where they will hopefully shrink down to my size. I give my husband full marks for effort and I am very grateful that I will have something cozy and comfy to wear, eventually. It certainly fits a lot better than the dental floss!

Bikini beach

My husband and I have been travelling together for the past twenty-some years, since we met. I have been travelling my whole life. From my very first trip from small-town Ontario to the big city, I have loved every part of exploring a new place.

In Grade 2, I wrote about my Christmas holiday when my parents initiated what would become an annual tradition. We were taken to Toronto and stayed at the Lord Simcoe Hotel, located at King and Simcoe Streets. The hotel has been long since demolished, but the memories remain forever. I was delighted with the big city lights that flashed on and off all night long. Mesmerized, I sat in my pajamas at the window looking out on the city most of the night.

In my story for school, I told how delighted I was that our room came complete with a bathroom, my other fascination on that trip. Okay, we have to give a very naïve seven-year-old a break here. Somewhere in my mother's boxes in our basement, this story still resides alongside my letter home from camp complaining that my older sister found playing jacks far more interesting than comforting her homesick sibling who had come to her cabin for a visit. Annoying, these younger siblings. Yes, it was a charmed life. I can see that now, and I can appreciate it as I watch our own children struggle to raise their youngsters.

I have travelled far and wide since that first trip to the big city. Funny how a hotel room complete with bathroom can fascinate a youngster, and how some sixty years later, a beach's proximity to a bathroom can still be so important.

On a recent trip to the islands for a week to get my exhausted husband out of his office and us away from the constant media barrage about Covid, we took our fully vaccinated selves off to catch up on sleep and soak up some sun, fully lathered in SPF 50 sunscreen and sheltering under a palapa beach hut.

I looked at all the very young bikini-clad women on the beach who arrived on their first day so pale and hours later at the dinner table were lobster red. What was even more astounding to me was to find them back on the beach the very next day, soaking up more sun by the water's edge. As anyone who has spent time frolicking in the waves will tell you, the sun is so much stronger when you are on the water, and we watched in dismay as the young folk got redder and redder day by day. And drunker and drunker too.

It's hard to look back at our younger selves and remember all our naïveté when we thought we were so invincible. The snowstorms in which we blithely borrowed the family car with no hint of fear that the roads might be icy. The total disregard for the middle eastern sun on a beach at the Red Sea, where my sister and I lay out for just one more hour after sunbathing for six with no sunscreen on. I remember my doctor cousin patching our shoulders and arms with Vietnam cream, a remedy that must grow off over weeks. How we fought the next day over who would suffer in the window seat of the bus with the sun shining on burnt skin on the return trip to the city. We both still have the scars from our stupidity.

It all looks so different from the other end of the age spectrum. The young folk at this all-inclusive resort were most concerned with how much alcohol they could consume with complete abandon. We, who are not big drinkers, just lay in the shade of our palapa figuring out how far the bathroom was and how much water we would need to stay properly hydrated. Someone once said to me that the lessons our parents don't teach us, life somehow does. How true.

The thing about travelling later in life is that what made you so excited in your youth can trigger fond remembrances. I for one have no desire to walk the plank on a booze-cruise pirate ship while friends film every minute of it for Instagram, praying that the top of a skimpy bikini won't abandon me in mid-flight. Yes, those days are definitely behind me, not that I ever did that. I prefer my sail and snorkel to be far more subdued. Of course, I still wave to those piling aboard the booze-cruising buses as they try to see how many of the local bars they can visit in one evening. I even sing along with the overly inebriated ones who climb aboard the shuttle that runs from one hotel to another: "Ole, Ole, Ole, Ole!" But it is with a more distant perspective and, frankly, relief at not being that age anymore.

I'm far more apt to ask for a quiet location for our room, where we won't be awakened by eager little ones clambering to go to the pool when they wake up at 6 a.m. Maybe when they are yours they are cute, but for others, definitely not.

While the young folk are out partying, we old folk are curled up in bed watching what we might watch on television back home. That is if there's no fire eating, limbo dancing or barbecuing on the beach to watch. Watching is much more fun than participating at this point. That we can still do.

Even the waves aren't as enticing as they used to be. When we were young, we just jumped in, frolicking and leaping over the roiling waters. Now we wonder if we will be knocked off our feet completely; we empathize with those pulling themselves ashore before they get washed back out. Do we miss the days of yore when we could run and jump and play? Not one little bit. That's what grandkids are for and ours are coming over this weekend. Now I am off to physiotherapy to deal with the effects of one rogue wave that had no respect for seniors.

"I don't buy green bananas"

As I have mentioned, when my mom passed away some twelve years ago, I inherited her friends — or perhaps adopted them is more accurate. As an able-bodied daughter of their late friend, I felt I had a duty to check in on them, to make sure they had enough food in the larder, so to speak. I would take them for groceries or to the hairdresser. I would drive one to synagogue religiously (how appropriate), pick up prescriptions, and just be an all-round dogsbody should they need. Medical appointments? No problem. I drove. A visit to an elderly friend in a retirement or nursing home? I visited them too because chances were pretty good that if they were a former friend of a friend of my mother's, my mom knew their friends too.

I was welcomed at very senior birthday parties and included on many occasions as an honorary member of the family. One hundredth birthday celebrations? I was there. Even if it meant skipping out of work and going halfway across town. My mom's friends made me feel welcome and they made sure their families knew how helpful I had been. And they reminded me of the wonderful friendships my mom had cultivated. In their stories and memories, a little bit of her lived on.

Sadly, most of these senior seniors have since passed. Maybe they are all reunited in the great beyond. When I would ask one friend I'll call Carol how she was doing she would reply, "Well, let's just say I don't buy green bananas." That stopped me in my tracks and I had to actually puzzle it out. I remember when I was doing my mom's shopping, if I bought bananas all of the same ripeness, she would say to me, "Oh, darling. How will I ever eat all these at the same time? There are far too many." Fortunately, she went on to seize the teachable moment and explained that when buying bananas, you must buy two for today and tomorrow, two more for later in the week and then two more that are green and will ripen in time for the following week. Who knew there was a science to buying bananas?

I discovered that if you watch closely in the produce department, you see banana mavens doing exactly that. They take two fairly ripe bananas from one bunch and then move on to a bunch that is less ripe and take two more, and so on. It must be a thing. Even I do it now, as I love bananas too. Ah, the wisdom of those who have gone before us.

So, when Carol exclaimed that she did not buy green bananas, it got me thinking. She obviously meant she might not be around to eat the green bananas by the time they ripened. I pondered, "What a pessimistic thought." I'm sure she was just being funny, but I still wanted to reassure her with something like "oh, don't be silly, of course you'll be here." But then, when you are ninety-eight, maybe you have seen a lot, lived a lot and you are just more pragmatic. On the other hand, if you come from good genes and expect to live a long life, then by all means, buy green bananas.

Carol passed away two years ago. My aunt passed away this past year. Little by little, my seniors are leaving this earth. And these were accomplished women who were head of their city's chapter of Hadassah-WIZO. One was a nursery schoolteacher. One a lawyer. Some had travelled all over the world and had apartments full of artifacts to prove it. They had raised families, had grandchildren and great grandchildren. They had watched future generations come into their own and in turn contribute to society as university and college professors, economists, and all manner of brilliant writers, producers, psychologists and the like. Of course, there was the odd offspring who never amounted to much and had given them a bit of grief, but by and large they had a lot that made them feel proud.

They must have felt gratified by the legacy they would leave and satisfied by their successes. However, when it was time to go and leave it all behind, they must have sensed that too. I hope I make the best of the years remaining to me. If genetics have anything to say about it, I will be around for a good long time. For now, I am indeed buying green bananas. However, heeding another lesson from my mother, I'll be sure to buy riper ones for the more immediate future too.

Speaking of legacies

The Queen just passed away. Just today. Just over an hour ago, and I am incredibly saddened. I feel as if I have lost a favourite relative I have known for many, many years. She has been a beneficent being who has been with me my entire life. She literally became queen at the time I was born. I grew up with Queen Elizabeth and she was right up there with the people I most admired and respected throughout my life. She was on every grade-school classroom wall. When I was bored to tears, I would stare up at Queen E and she would always smile down on me. I would smile back and wonder how heavy her crown was and did it dig in like my barrettes did? Every morning we sang "God Save the Queen" because we were part of the British Empire.

In my opinion, she was every bit a lady. A true lady. More importantly, she was the real deal. A kind, caring human being who kept it all together. Grace under pressure. When the world was raging at war, she kept calm. She was a reassuring presence that everything would turn out all right. She was the epitome of "Keep calm and carry on." Though the pinnacle of polite society, she always had a twinkle in her eye and a sense of humour. She was honourable and worked her whole life in service to others.

How many people can say that about their lives at the end? The fact that she loved dogs and horses must have meant they knew the good inside her, as animals are so known to do. What a legacy.

Let's hope she imparted a sense of wisdom, perspective, good judgment and commitment to her offspring. Of course, offspring are always another story, no matter who you are. Why, even the Queen of England had her challenges. It was unusual for someone at the top of the pecking order — and, let's face it, how much higher can you go — to have *tsouris* from *kinder* (Yiddish for grief from children). And she certainly had her share of it, which, to me, made her one of us.

I'm sure if she was playing baseball out in the schoolyard with us, everyone would pick her first to be on their baseball team, and as someone who rarely got picked, I consider that a very high honour.

The fact that she immersed herself in her duties as figurehead of the British Empire, always with grace and poise and a genuine interest in others, didn't seem to make her that different from all of us. Yes, she had many palaces, but I used to think it would be like us going to the cottage.

What made Queen E seem so approachable was that she always seemed like she was head of the flock and we were her sheep. We looked up to her. We admired her. She never in her life used the word "I" when referring to herself. She preferred "one" as in "one just doesn't do that, does one?" It was never a case of she, the Queen, and we the commoners. We were her loyal subjects and yet she would always accept our gifts and flowers with such genuine warmth and a smile for everyone.

If I was asked who in the world I would like to meet, I would wish to have met or had high tea with Queen E. I know she would have made me feel comfortable. After getting over the curtsying and the deference that must be shown, it would have been just like having tea with your own grandma. So I think. I also think her children and grandchildren were very lucky to have the time they had with her. How wonderful to know your bubby and zadie well into your adult years as grandchildren.

There's something mysterious about never having known my father's parents, who had passed on by the time I was born. I guess in my mind I replaced my real grandmother with Queen Elizabeth. I kept her in this lofty place in my heart, and now that she too has passed, there is one more missing piece in my so-called family.

Not yet

It was a Thursday morning Zumba Gold class at our local community centre. Gold, as in for seniors. Ah yes, the golden years. I suspected I was one of the youngest in this class. The community centre had a vibrant and thriving seniors' program, with everything from pickleball to ballroom and line dancing, painting classes and bridge tournaments. For variety, they took a group of seniors by bus to the Stratford Theatre Festival, and had high teas at a local historical home. The lounge area was hopping, and there was always a full slate of activities going on.

I wasn't 100 percent sure I was old enough to be part of the Zumba class, though various body parts had started to complain and I was assured it was perfect for me. I loved Zumba from the very first class before Covid struck and everything was shut down for the better part of two years. I loved the instructor and felt right at home. Okay, the nine o'clock start was not a favourite of mine as I have a dog to walk first, and half the fun of being retired is not having to be up so early each day. On the other hand, the class was always well attended by those who regularly get up at 6 a.m. just because.

Having made it through Covid unscathed, and still wearing a mask inside grocery stores and other places where people congregate in numbers, I was somewhat hesitant when the notice came out that classes were once again going to be held in person. You had to show proof of vaccination but dancing without a mask was permitted.

I had spent Covid doing Zumba online in the three feet of space between my dining room and my living room not covered by carpet, mostly with the blinds closed so no one would have to witness my cavorting. Even the dog closed her eyes to the sight of her ancient and honourable mistress dancing like a complete fool as I went through the requisite steps and tried to avoid banging into the walls or the furniture. To get my iPad up high enough to see the instructor, I had it balanced on two Christmas cookie tins — you know, the kind you buy for yourself but never admit to having in the house. They were the chief reason I should be working out at Zumba.

Needless to say, returning in person to class was an experience. I recognized perhaps two of my former dancing seniors and a whole lot more who were obviously much older than I, or so I thought. At 11:30, the new start time, the place was packed. My spot in the second row was still there and the new instructor was fantastic. I was delighted to be on my feet salsa-ing away. The music was uplifting and fun and the energy in the class and from the instructor, who smiled at us non-stop, was wonderful. After class there was an announcement that a treat would be available in the lounge. Thinking, "Aha, here is a way to access a limited sampling of Hallowe'en goodies," off I went to blithely undo all the good I had just done my body in class.

To my amazement, who was offering goodies to us seniors but a local retirement residence where I had not so long ago installed my ninety-four-year-old mother-in-law and ninety-seven-year-old father-in-law. When my father-in-law fell four years ago and could no longer live in his split-level home, it seemed like a good idea to get them moved in. Finding the retirement residence staff awaiting our arrival with treats and spinning a prize wheel was too much. I had to tell them who I was and that, no, I was not ready to consider moving in. I was not that generation.

But am I? I'm sure some of my Zumba pals might be delighted to make that next move. Not I. Not now. Not for another thirty years. Okay, maybe twenty years. This was a rude awakening, to be sure, and it didn't help when everyone asked me, "When is your husband retiring?" "Not yet," I said. "He's happy doing what he's doing. Maybe in a few years." That's probably what I should have told the well-meaning youngsters who were spinning the wheel for prizes. I have to hand it to them. It was a great marketing strategy. Just not for me. After all I'm not that old, not yet. It's not my time.

Is it pajama time yet?

From the moment we are born, our world gets bigger and bigger, one experience at a time. Each day brings new adventures and capabilities. We spend our lives becoming independent. Then, at some point, the process starts to reverse. First, we lose our balance, then our memories, then our hearing, our eyesight and eventually our independence, so we are almost right back at the beginning. A rather depressing thought, to be sure. While it doesn't happen in the space of a paragraph, at some point we realize we aren't as capable as we were just a short time ago and, predictably, our world and daily life start to shrink.

In a conversation with a close friend with whom I chat daily, we were having a discussion about how the combination of getting older and the days getting shorter conspire to make us want to stay at home. We were commenting on the fact that the older we get, the harder it is to do all the things we used to do in a day without even thinking twice.

And then we acknowledged the nights when we struggle to fall asleep. We have begun to get up a few times during the night for that trip to the bathroom. Getting back to sleep and staying asleep is a whole other challenge. I'm not sure if, as we age, we have less energy because we don't sleep, or we don't need as much sleep because we're doing less. It is a conundrum. I can lie awake for hours enumerating all the body parts that hurt. (Ah, that organ recital.) And finding a position that doesn't hurt is a challenge as well. No wonder some of my friends have started sleeping later and going to bed earlier.

I guess as we age there are fewer things we need, and want, to do. When the weather does not cooperate and the days get shorter, I try to get the dog walked twice and all errands done before it starts to get dark. How quickly I have forgotten the days when I walked the dog at 6 a.m. to be at work by 8 and how, for many years, I came home in the dark all winter.

Not long ago, I heard that the price of gas was going to drop in the evening and off I went at about 8 p.m. to fill the tank. How surprised was I to discover there's a whole world out there — traffic, lights and people shopping and doing all kinds of things. At 8 p.m. at night!

My friend was out with her husband for a drive one late morning and I jokingly asked if she was already longing for her pajamas. She often does her errands, goes for a swim and then, if she has no plans to go anywhere, she will put on her pajamas and be cozy. She laughed and said, no, she was meeting a friend for coffee later so the pajamas would have to wait. Well, good for her for pushing the envelope.

I find myself no longer envying youth and all the trials and tribulations they will face. I'm quite content with what I have accomplished and my goals are far less physically demanding. I'm just hoping I can hang on to my mental faculties long enough to say I did it all, and enjoyed it.

A good chunk of my days are now spent walking into rooms and wondering "What was it I came in here to do?" Never mind. I am sure I will find many projects left undone from another day and time when I suddenly remembered something else that needed my attention.

The value of an experiential learner

Some people learn by listening, some by reading. Others learn by doing — just jumping right in at the deep end. Keeping up with changes in technology is a bit like that. Sure, there were lots of bright minds who wrote code to program the early computers, but in the 1990s when computers first showed up at work, no one really knew what they were about. Rather than take a course, I just started hitting keys and buttons until I figured it out. Maybe I was just not good at following instructions. My husband says that's so.

I remember once putting together a stand for our television while my daughter watched. It didn't resemble the instructions or the picture of the finished product. "Take it back," my daughter urged. "Bring home another one and I will help you." I did what she suggested and darned if she didn't have the whole thing put together, glass door, shelves and all, in about fifteen minutes. I was blown away. How did she do that? I guess, as was foretold in tests from elementary school, she was very good at visual abstract sequencing. She knew exactly how this TV stand should be assembled before we even started laying out all the pieces. Would that all of life was that easy.

My husband insists to this day that I am too quick to push buttons, especially computer keys. In fact, I once sent a very incriminating email to the one person I did not want to receive it. That's called learning the hard way. A hard one to live down too.

I have been told good judgment comes from experience and experience comes from bad judgment, so I guess there are times when I'm not the only experiential learner. How much do I learn from something I do right? Not much. Screwing up is a far greater learning experience. When I make a mistake and have to take many steps to fix it, that is a learning opportunity. Maybe that is what is meant by carpe diem. Seize the day, or the teachable moment.

I have to admit, I kind of admire the get-'er-done kind of people. They just jump in and figure it out as they go along. We don't always get a road map or illustrated instructions with steps A and B to guide us. Sure, these instructions will help us when we are assembling furniture, but sometimes it's more about diving right in when life is offering so many choices. I just want to get started on a path, any path, even if it takes a leap of faith.

One of my mother's favourite poems, in fact the one we read at her gravestone unveiling, was Robert Frost's "The Road Less Travelled."

> Two roads diverged in a wood, and I —
> I took the one less travelled by,
> And that has made all the difference.

How different one's life turns out because of a path chosen or a decision made, sometimes on the spur of the moment. When I started university, I had no clue where I would end up or what

I would do with my life. Mostly the pieces just fell into place as I went along. Of course, Stephen Covey in his *Seven Habits of Highly Effective People* would say, "If you don't have your own agenda, you will become part of someone else's." That may well be true... And then there was the time our GPS told us exactly where to go and we ended up in someone's backyard instead of on the road to a golf course. That was definitely a road less travelled, and probably not appreciated by the homeowner.

A final thought on aging, a curiosity all its own

"Beauty is in the eye of the beholder," isn't that what they say? And as my first mother-in-law once reminded me, "Make new friends but keep the old. One is silver, the other gold." So much wisdom contained in those words. If only I had listened to my elders more.

My dad once told me that at his twenty-fifth medical school reunion one of his friends opined, "The years have been kind to you." What an interesting way of putting it. Brilliant in fact. If someone said that to me, I would feel positively ... ancient. And just how kind have those years been? With all we go through by the time we get to our senior years (and I'm not even at my senior, senior years, as I call them) it's a miracle we resemble anything of our earlier selves. Granted, I still see that mischievous twinkle in my eye when I look in the mirror. But what do others see? Do they see the joy I feel at being alive and finally able to live life the way I want? Do they see how spry I feel?

After years of Covid lurking like an ever-present darkness —a killjoy ready to take away our friends and family members at worst, and at best our hard-won freedom — it was like being let out of school early to get together with those we've been missing. By the time we could again see friends we have known for many years (at mostly outside gatherings just to be safe), I noticed how much older everyone looked. I saw many wrinkles. I saw drawn and worn faces. I saw the worry in friends' eyes. The passage of time had not been good to all of us.

Time leaves its marks. My husband now has a permanent crease between his eyes from the constant worry of watching the health-care system he has so dedicatedly served for over forty-five years collapse before us. I see his reluctance to let go of his lifelong medical practice and take the next step in his life. Having retired some years before him, I am delighted to have all the time to do those activities I most wanted to do all the years I was working. I loved my career, but it was time to do something else, and now I delight in taking courses, painting, writing, reading and golfing. Travelling was not always something we could afford to do when we were young and struggling, but we can now. Spending time with grandchildren is so wonderful. And waking up late when I have had a not-so-great night is a gift. Getting together with friends and family and spending time doing the things I love to do most, with those I love most, is wonderful.

When I look into the curiosity cabinet of my life and see all the wonderful memories on my shelves, I am truly grateful. It holds interesting curiosities too, some funny, others sad, some even terrifying from the perspective of an adult many years later. These curiosities have made me who I am.

What a shame we don't share more of who we are with our children and their children. It's important that they know we were not always the sophisticated, aging, sometimes creaking adults they see before them. We too had fears and joys, laughter and tears, mischief and humour, and even though we look so much older on the outside, we are still the same human beings on the inside.

It's sad but true that everyone is so busy living their own lives that they don't take the time to ask us about our lives — not just our lives today, but long ago. And not sarcastically, as in, "So how was it back in the Dark Ages, when you didn't have cell phones and computers?" I would love to answer, "It was marvelous. We actually listened when people spoke to us and when they asked us questions, we answered without texting, WhatsApping or TikToking." Imagine that. I wonder what they will be writing about some thirty or forty years from now.

Technology has brought many wonderful, head-spinning new ideas and customs, and we now have generations who have spent every waking moment benefiting from them. Younger generations can only imagine what their dotage will feel like; maybe they will remember how they teased us when we didn't catch on to the latest tech gadgets right away. It's true that to remain in touch with their world we have to get with the program and expand our skills. But let's hope we don't completely lose all that was so wonderful in our world before technology took off like a shot.

I guess getting older is the revenge of past generations, a conspiracy of seniors, if you will. Those of us who thought we were so hip and cool never dreamed that the doddering old fools on the outer edges of the bar or bat mitzvah dance floor, the ones we barely tolerated, happily sitting as far as possible from the noisy speakers, really knew a thing or two about life. Now, we are the ones giving the next generations the cash gifts to help fuel and finance their dreams. If only it were possible to bridge the gap and say, "We, too, have been where you are. Enjoy it. You'll be sitting over here soon enough."

Acknowledgements

No book writes itself and I have many people to thank for their insight, wisdom, support, humour and knowledge.

To Judy Cipin, who is without doubt the best listener of my stories and who believed in my ability to tell them with humour and accuracy. I would not have even attempted a second chapter without your support and laughter. Thank you for encouraging me to keep writing.

To my readers, Eleanor Minuk and Barbara Snelgrove, thank you for your friendship and wisdom, and the keen eyes through which you see how to make my stories better.

To my cherished and talented editor, Marial Shea, for laughing along with me through my crazy tales and making them so much more relatable and enjoyable. I treasure your belief in me and your ability to make words sing and dance.

To Tania Craan and Jan Westendorp for your talent and creativity in bringing the book to life in print and e-format.

To my family and friends, who humour me, help me in my attempts to humour you, the reader, and convince me to keep at it. Thank you for your input, ideas and steadfast support.

To my husband, who allows me to relay our stories with cheerful good will and always makes sure I don't exaggerate in the recounting of Tales. For your steady calm and ongoing love and support and for never minding as I disappear sometimes in the middle of dinner to capture an amusing anecdote and return hours later, you have my gratitude and love.

Thank you to my readers for indulging me and laughing along with me while sharing the many foibles and quirks of this crazy world in which we live.

About the Author

Marjie Zacks grew up in Peterborough and Ottawa, Ontario. She has a B.A. in Sociology from York University and a Master of Education from Central Michigan University, and is the author of *It All Ends Up in A Parfait Glass: A Tribute to My Mother's Wisdom*. Her second book, *Tales from the Curio Cabinet*, is her "somewhat autobiographical" perspective on life. Marjie has four grown children and three not-so-grown grandchildren. She lives in the Toronto area with her husband and their much loved and very spoiled but adorable four-footed sidekick, Winnie.

www.ingramcontent.com/pod-product-compliance
Lightning Source LLC
Chambersburg PA
CBHW021110080526
44587CB00010B/464